GARLAND STUDIES ON

THE ELDERLY IN AMERICA

A collection of monographs and dissertations addressing specific problems facing the elderly in a changing America

EDITED BY
STUART BRUCHEY
Columbia University

A Garland Series

EVELINE M. BURNS AND THE AMERICAN SOCIAL SECURITY SYSTEM 1935-1960

Linda R. Wolf Jones

GARLAND PUBLISHING
New York & London
1991

Appendix I is reprinted from Social Security in International Perspective: Essays in Honor of Eveline M. Burns with the kind permission of Columbia University Press.

Appendix IV is reprinted from Toward Social Security with the kind permission of McGraw-Hill.

Library of Congress Cataloging-in-Publication Data

Jones, Linda R. Wolf.
Eveline M. Burns and the American Social Security system, 1935-1960 / Linda R. Wolf Jones
p. cm. — (Garland studies on the elderly in America)
Includes bibliographical references and index.
ISBN 0-8153-0523-0
1. Old age pensions—United States—History. 2. Social security—United States—History. 3. Burns, Eveline Mabel Richardson, 1900- .
I. Title. II. Series.
HD7105.35.U6J66 1991
368.4'3'00973—dc20

91-30447
CIP

Printed on acid-free 250-year-life paper

MANUFACTURED IN THE UNITED STATES OF AMERICA

DEDICATION

To my daughter, Elisabeth Noel Jones; my grandmother, Mollie Pinkowitz; and my friend, Eveline M. Burns -- each, in her own way, a strong, intelligent and independent woman

ACKNOWLEDGMENTS

This study--which was undertaken as a doctoral dissertation at the Wurzweiler School of Social Work, Yeshiva University--would not have been possible without the cooperation and support of Dr. Eveline M. Burns. To her and to Dr. Louis Levitt, who advised the study, I owe my deep thanks and unbounded gratitude. Dr. Eli Levy and Dr. Norman Linzer reviewed the study in addition to Dr. Levitt; I am grateful to them for their assistance. Any errors of fact or interpretation, however, are mine alone.

I am also grateful for the support and tolerance of friends, relatives and colleagues during the years of research and writing. In particular, I could not have completed the work were it not for the patience and understanding of my daughter, Elisabeth Noel Jones.

Faith, and the memory of loved ones who had faith in me, kept me going when the work seemed endless and the sunshine streaming in the windows competed with the typewriter for my attention.

TABLE OF CONTENTS

LIST OF APPENDICES

INTRODUCTION

In Memoriam: Eveline M. Burns
(March 16, 1900 - September 3, 1985)

Dr. Eveline M. Burns was a model of professional leadership for more than fifty years. She worked tirelessly in the field of social policy--as a writer, a professor, an advisor, an analyst and an advocate--for most of her lifetime. She was involved with major social welfare legislation, concentrating in large part on income security and related issues, since the inception of the Social Security Act in 1935. This study represents an opportunity to examine some of her work, including both her writings and her other professional activities and associations, from the perspective of her sustained efforts to influence social policy. Specifically, the study explores her attempts to influence social policy through a multiplicity of approaches, both direct and indirect, particularly with respect to old age retirement income. The study's foundation is Dr. Burns' lifelong exercise of professional leadership.

The study covers the period from 1935 to 1960, a twenty-five year time frame in which there were major shifts in economic and social conditions and the political climate as well as major changes in domestic economic and social legislation. The *zeitgeist* of those years is therefore depicted and old age retirement legislation in the Social Security program between 1935 and 1960 is traced. The descriptions of historical trends and events and the legislative changes help to place Dr. Burns' work in a broader context. Her carefully thought-out policy positions stayed relatively constant, however, and remained relevant even as times changed.

The professional life of this remarkable woman

has not yet received much attention in the social work literature. The present study constitutes, in essence, an appreciation of her extensive professional contribution, focusing here on her work on Social Security old age retirement issues from 1935 to 1960. It represents what I believe to be the first in-depth look at some aspects of her life and work.

I was able to share the completed study with Dr. Burns in the summer of 1985, shortly before her death. She was clearly pleased with the work and with the realization that her life story--what she did and how she did it--would not be lost to future generations of scholars and others interested in Social Security and social welfare issues. I told her at that time, and continue to believe, that the present study may be the first research investigation into her life and work, but that it will not be the last.

PART ONE

CONTEXT OF THE STUDY

CHAPTER I

THE FRAME OF REFERENCE

Focus for the Inquiry: How Eveline M. Burns Worked to Influence the Development of National Income Security Policy

Eveline M. Burns is well known in the social work profession as a social economist, professor, lecturer and author in the field of social policy in general and income security in particular. She was a Professor of Social Work at the Columbia University School of Social Work for over twenty years (1946-1967). Prior to that time, she had already spent over fifteen years as a faculty member at the London School of Economics and the Columbia University Economics Department and had served in several key government advisory roles on income security issues, participating in planning for both the original Social Security Act of 1935 and the directions which the nation might take in the post-World War II era. This study examines how Dr. Burns, as a professional social welfare consultant and educator, used those roles to try to influence national income security policy in the period from 1935 to 1960, from the beginning of a national income security policy in the United States through its first quarter century.

The year 1935 was a watershed in the history of American social policy with respect to societal concern for the income security of its individual members.[1] The passage of the Social Security Act in that year opened doors domestically to new policies, programs, and concepts about personal and social responsibility. The 1935 legislation represented the

---

[1] "Social policy" is discussed conceptually in a later part of this chapter. The reader is directed to the section on "Significance of the Focus of the Inquiry," pp. 9-14, for a discussion of the term and its use in this study.

first comprehensive effort in this country to identify basic elements of income security, to develop a federal policy to deal with them, and to incorporate the pieces of that policy into a single, far-reaching act of law.[2] Over the following decades, both the size and scope of the programs were expanded considerably through amendments to the Act.

The four major individual income security needs which were addressed in the original Social Security Act and subsequently refined in amendments are old age retirement, unemployment, family assistance and disability. This study focuses on the issues related to old age retirement: how Dr. Burns viewed them and worked to shape the enactment of legislation. The choice of the issues centering on old age retirement income was guided by several factors. First, it is the issue area in which Dr. Burns worked most consistently over the course of her professional career. Second, it is an area in which national social policies, the legislation affecting the policies, and efforts to influence the policies can be more clearly isolated for analysis, since there are no individual state-by-state variations to cloud the picture. Finally, it has been the most widespread of the four issue areas and has, over the long term, directly touched the lives of the greatest number of people. It is therefore a significant area of study for the present purpose.

In 1935, Eveline M. Burns was a thirty-five-year-old, British-trained economist with career credentials in both academia and government. She was, in fact, one of the staff members of the Committee on Economic Security created by President Franklin D. Roosevelt to draft social security

---

[2] The rationale for the original (i.e., 1935) legislation was anchored in the Preamble to the United States Constitution, which sanctioned taking action "to promote the general welfare." The stated purpose of the Social Security Act of 1935, as expressed in the first words of that legislation, is: "To provide for the general welfare. . . ."

legislation, which culminated in the Social Security Act.[3] From the passage of that Act forward, she literally devoted a lifetime to thinking, writing, speaking and teaching about the social and economic issues which it addressed, the policies which it promoted, and the programs which it established and introduced into routine American life.

Many of Dr. Burns' writings, including several of her best-known books, deal with the income security needs of individuals and families and the ways in which federal policies and law act to meet or fail to meet those needs. She writes about these issues in a framework of policy analysis, within which she presents facts and analyzes arguments in order to explain the issues and alternatives and to point out and advise on the likely consequences of one or another course of action. The present inquiry will examine, through Dr. Burns' writings and her other career-related activities, how she sought to influence income security legislation dealing with old age retirement policies and programs between the years 1935 and 1960. It describes her use of not only her writings, but also of her professional positions (government consultant, professor, officer in professional organizations and associations) to advance her views.

Major legislation does not take place in a vacuum; it is enacted against a backdrop of historical events and prevailing conditions and conflicting social, economic and political forces. Policy analysis must take these actual conditions into consideration while simultaneously using a

---

[3] The issue of social insurance began to receive increasing attention in the early 1930s, with both advocates and opponents of such measures actively pressing their positions with government officials and the public. In mid-1934, President Roosevelt expressed his own desire for a sound social insurance program, laid down some general principles, and appointed a Committee on Economic Security to formulate and submit a program to him before the end of the calendar year.

theoretical perspective to move from a statement of present issues and relationships to an anticipation of how they might evolve. The present inquiry examines the Burnsian analyses of old age retirement issues and her advocacy of changes in policies and legislation in terms of their relationship to real world conditions. It looks at changes in both national legislative policies and her analyses of and attempts to influence those policies over time. It examines them within the theoretical framework of institutional change influenced by professional leadership.

We seek to learn through this study, by using the focusing lens of Dr. Burns' career, how a single social work professional can utilize her expert skills and positions within the profession to influence professional and public opinion on the direction of national social policy. The timeframe, 1935 through 1960, allows us to see the inception and maturing of old age retirement policies over a key quarter century. A redirection of national attention took place after 1960 to focus primarily on poverty and health issues; the main expansions of the income portions of the old age retirement program had, however, taken place by that time.

This study contributes to the knowledge of the social work profession by providing a model of how an individual practitioner in roles of potential influence can carry out his professional purpose and fulfill his ethical responsibility in the realm of social policy. According to Charles Levy, the professional purpose "is to help his clientele relate itself productively to its own preferred aspirations, or institutionally assigned objectives, and to its social environment to the extent that the environment affects or is affected by his clientele's aspirations."[4] In carrying out that purpose, "if social conditions and social policies are the barrier

---

[4] Charles S. Levy, "Putting the Social Work Back into Social Work," Journal of Jewish Communal Service 51 (Winter 1974): 171.

to the clientele's social fulfillment or social productivity, the social work focus is on social and policy change."[5] In addition to professional purpose, the practitioner's ethical responsibility is

> to make use of his professional knowledge and skill in behalf of mankind in general, particularly that segment of it which is unduly disadvantaged. . . . From an ethical point of view, the practitioner is not finished when he has closed a client's case, for individual cases inductively lead to the perception of general needs to which his professional competence is relevant, and to which he owes acknowledged responsibility to apply himself.[6]

Leadership in the social policy arena provides a means for a social work professional to apply himself to general needs.

In its conceptualization of the work of Dr. Burns, this study offers a model of professional leadership for current and future social work practitioners who seek to influence social policy as part of their mandated professional purpose and ethical responsibility. The study of her exercise of professional leadership will guide and assist in the education of future leaders and others who aspire to influence social policy from within the social welfare institution.

Significance of the Focus of the Inquiry

Social welfare policy is an elusive and complicated subject for social work practitioners. "Students entering the field of social welfare policy quickly come to feel somewhat like Alice at the

---

[5] Ibid., p. 175.

[6] Charles S. Levy, "Professional Ethics as Humanistic Ethics," Jewish Social Work Forum 9 (Spring 1972): 11.

Queen's croquet party."[7] The rules for policymaking and the actions of policy makers not only appear unclear, but in fact are unclear much of the time. Nevertheless, it is important to try to understand policies and policymaking within a rational framework.

> The process by which a social policy is formulated is highly complex and dynamic. Thus it is very difficult to describe or explain, but social workers who seek in one way or another to change the social order must strive for some sort of comprehension.[8]

Even those social work professionals who do not seek social change directly benefit from an understanding of social welfare policy. Gilbert and Specht have stated that

> the study of this subject matter is central for those who practice in the social services because, to a large extent, it shapes the forms of practice that professionals are called upon to use and determines the client systems to be served.[9]

One difficulty in coming to an understanding of social welfare policy is that there is no professionally agreed-upon definition of the term. One review of the use of the term "social policy" (which is generally used by social welfare professionals in referring to social welfare policy,

---

[7] Neil Gilbert and Harry Specht, Dimensions of Social Welfare Policy (Englewood Cliffs, N.J.: Prentice-Hall, Inc., 1974), p. 1.

[8] Joseph Heffernan and Barbara Turnan, "Searching the Literature," in Social Work Research and Evaluation, ed. Richard M. Grinnell, Jr. (Itasca, Ill.: F.E. Peacock Publishers, Inc., 1981), p. 46.

[9] Gilbert and Specht, p.1.

a practice which I will follow in this study) leads to the conclusion that "it lacks a commonly accepted, universally valid definition."[10] David Gil suggests that a "formal, universally valid definition" would be:

> Social policies are principles or courses of action designed to influence (1) the overall quality of life in a society; (2) the circumstances of living of individuals and groups in that society; and (3) the nature of intra-societal relationships among individuals, groups, and society as a whole.[11]

Such a far-reaching definition, however precise, is too broad to be of practical use for social workers in informing their policy activities. Definitions proposed by Charles Levy and by Eveline Burns herself are more useful. To Levy, a policy is "a system of value decisions to guide planning and action regarding an identified need or problem"; a social policy is one which goes beyond a specific client or clients to affect general classes of people.[12] Dr. Burns, in a speech urging more professional attention to social policy on the part of social workers, defined it as "the organized efforts of society to meet identifiable personal needs of, or social problems presented by, groups or individuals."[13]

---

[10] David G. Gil, Unravelling Social Policy: Theory, Analysis and Political Action Towards Social Equality (Cambridge, Mass.: Schenkman Publishing Co., 1973), p.3.

[11] Ibid., p.24.

[12] Charles S. Levy, "The Social Worker as Agent of Policy Change," Social Casework 51 (February 1970): 103.

[13] Eveline M. Burns, "Social Policy: The Stepchild of the Curriculum," in Proceedings of Ninth Annual Program Meeting, Council on Social Work Education (New York: Council on Social Work Education, 1961), pp. 23-34.

Although both of these definitions refer to identified needs and problems without explanation of those latter terms, they are nevertheless adequate and clear statements for understanding what directs social policy.

Analysis of social policies is necessary in order to understand their impact on the well-being of individuals from a social work perspective. The significance of social policy analysis as a form of social work practice within the institution of social welfare has been greatly enhanced by the work of Eveline M. Burns. "Their [Eveline M. Burns and Richard M. Titmuss] impact on this field is of such magnitude as to be pervasive and footnotes are an inadequate means of recognizing how much they have done to illumine social welfare policy."[14] Dr. Burns has been a farsighted individual in the social welfare field for more than a half century and one of this country's foremost social policy analysts for much of that time. Her contributions to social policy thought and analysis have played a large part in shaping the field. A concomitant issue, however, is whether and how an individual, however skilled in policy analysis, can work to have an impact on the development of social policy itself. The following chapters trace the old age retirement policies and provisions found in the Social Security Act legislation over the period 1935-1960 and compare the legislation enacted to the professional activities and writings of Eveline M. Burns during that time. The inquiry examines her efforts to influence policy change, both directly and indirectly.

It has frequently been stated that social work and social welfare professionals have an obligation to press for enlightened changes in public social welfare policies. According to the Code of Ethics of the National Association of Social Workers, "The

---

[14] Gilbert and Specht, p. xii. Richard M. Titmuss (1907-1973) was a leading English social scientist and professor and a contemporary of Dr. Burns.

social worker should advocate changes in policy and legislation to improve social conditions and to promote social justice."[15] As Charles Levy has put it,

> In an important sense, social work practice in general is a matter of shaping, selecting, or influencing policy. . . . For those individuals or groups whose fate rests on institutional or legislative choices, this means applying influence or pressure with the goal of establishing conditions most conducive to their well-being and development.[16]

The use of self to influence social policy can take one or both of two paths: individual action or group action. According to Charles Lindblom, "if a citizen wants to be an effective influence on policy and is not, as a scholar or journalist, strategically placed to make an individual contribution to analysis, he has to join forces with other citizens."[17] Both the individual and group routes require effort.

> Policy making is laborious; there is no escaping its burdens. For other than scholars, philosophers, and publicists whose ideas are powerful enough to influence policy at a distance (and even they have to work at the formulation and communication of their ideas), a big share in policy making is reserved to those who look at participating in the play of power not as a privilege but as a task, job, or

---

[15] National Association of Social Workers, The NASW Code of Ethics (as passed by the 1979 Delegate Assembly), section VI:P:6. (Reprint)

[16] Levy, "The Social Worker as Agent of Policy Change," p. 103.

[17] Charles E. Lindblom, The Policy-Making Process, Foundations of Modern Political Science Series (Englewood Cliffs, N.J.: Prentice-Hall, Inc., 1968), p. 49.

career.[18]

Dr. Burns chose to follow both routes. As a prominent scholar, she was "strategically placed to make an individual contribution to analysis" and to try "to influence policy at a distance" on the basis of her ideas. Nevertheless, she also sought and exercised professional interest-group leadership to provide information and to gather support for preferred policy positions.

This study examines Dr. Burns' work along both of these paths. It documents her efforts as a social work leader and educator to carry out as fully as possible the professional mandate of advocating changes in policy and legislation, using both individual and group means to do so. Such dual action is consistent with Levy's contention, for example, that social work faculty members have an obligation to act both individually as scholars and jointly as members of the institution "to insure that society is maximally responsive to its members most in need and most deprived."[19] One type of action, individual or group, does not negate the other; for social work scholars, both come under the rubric of professional responsibility. The study also shows how an individual in the social work field can use professional associations to catalyze interest, advance a policy agenda and provide leverage in the political arena on a chosen issue of concern.

Hypotheses

In order to trace and examine the methods used by Dr. Burns to try to influence national social policy, this study will utilize the following

---

[18] Ibid., p. 115.

[19] Charles S. Levy, "(The Graduate) School (of Social Work) and Society," Journal of Education for Social Work 7 (Spring 1971): 30.

hypotheses:

Hypothesis 1. Dr. Burns, through her position as a highly regarded consultant, professor, and member of professional organizations, was able to gain attention for her views on Social Security old age retirement and used those opportunities to provide a policy agenda on which others in, and outside of, the profession could focus and around which they could coalesce.

Hypothesis 2. Dr. Burns used her associations (advisory committees, schools of social work, professional organizations) as a power base for gathering support for the policy positions which she espoused.

Hypothesis 3. Dr. Burns was a political realist who understood how the legislative process functioned and accepted, but worked for change within, existing government, political and professional structures. She used her influence in the social work profession to urge continued legislative and policy change through the democratic process rather than espousing more radical changes in either policies or methods of attainment.

Theoretical Framework

The present study places Dr. Burns' work in a theoretical framework of the relationship of profession to institution: the profession is viewed as carrying responsibility for giving shape and direction to the institution in which it is anchored; this function is carried out through the individual and joint actions of its practitioners. The study examines Dr. Burns' work as a model of exemplary professional leadership in this regard. It presents background data regarding her life and the historical zeitgeist of the period under consideration (1935-1960). It tracks the old age retirement legislation enacted during the same years. Her writings and professional activities in those legislative subject areas are then examined in terms of the policy positions which she espoused, the means which she used to make preferred positions known and to gain attention for them, and her leadership role in professional associations and organizations as one means of garnering interest and support on policy issues. From the findings, the study will draw conclusions as to the influence which esteemed scholarly and professional status and activities may have had in this case on the direction of actual legislative change and the implications for other social work and social welfare leaders in their efforts to influence social policy.

The theoretical framework of this study utilizes a model of historical analysis built on: "a set of statements about how the world works which guides their [historians'] investigation."[20] The investigations undertaken in this study will be based on the concept of the relationship of profession to institution, in this case the work of a professional leader in social work to the institution of social welfare. Louis Levitt has defined the concept of institution as

> an organizing principle . . . encompassing the laws, regulations, roles, role expectations, norms, customs, organizations, occupations and particularized ideas related to the satisfaction of a critical societal need or function.[21]

In examining institutions, according to Levitt, "one is struck with the centrality of professions" and that "the functions performed by the professions include the direct provision of many of the important services provided by the institution as well as activities which shape, guide, lead and direct the

---

[20] Paul Stuart, "Historical Research," in Grinnell, p. 326.

[21] Louis Levitt, "Social Work and Social Welfare: A Conceptual Matrix," Journal of Sociology and Social Welfare 7 (September 1980): 637.

evolution of the institution."[22] Clarke Chambers likens these two distinct sets of functions in the social welfare institution, the provision of services and the provision of leadership, to the distinction in the religious institution between "priests" and "prophets." According to Chambers,

> the vast majority of professional social workers are properly engaged in what we may call priestly functions. The actionists, the prophets if you wish, are exceptional leaders--impatient with ameliorative measures, demanding social justice through social reform.[23]

Chambers, like Levitt, sees both functions as intrinsic to the responsibility of the social work profession within the social welfare institution, in that

> the two overlapping phases of social work continue to exist, not always harmoniously, but certainly in interdependence--the one focused on the individual and his welfare, strongly influenced by the psychological disciplines . . .; the other concerned with reform, with reconstruction, informed primarily by the social sciences . . . .[24]

It is the latter function and responsibility of the social work profession--that of providing leadership and direction to social welfare by envisioning ways in which society could be more just and advocating movement in that direction through social policy reform--which is the value base of this inquiry.

---

[22] Ibid., p. 639.

[23] Clarke A. Chambers, "An Historical Perspective on Political Action Vs. Individualized Treatment," in <u>Perspectives on Social Welfare: An Introductory Anthology</u>, ed. Paul E. Weinberger (London: The Macmillan Company, Collier-Macmillan Limited, 1969), pp. 92-93.

[24] Ibid., p. 92.

The leadership of the social work profession within the social welfare institution is particularly important because of the nature of that institution. Social welfare concerns itself with the needs of people who are weak, poor, powerless, or otherwise vulnerable. It must stand up for that population and help it to maintain its rights, its dignity and its means of subsistence in the face of competing demands and the prevailing values and attitudes of the larger society. That larger society can conceptualize the social welfare institution as an integral and essential part of the social framework or as an undesirable, but tolerated adjunct to it. The activities of the social work profession serve not only to influence the institution itself, but also to help shape the roles envisioned for social welfare by those outside of the institution and by society at large. In its helping role, social welfare may be thought of as integral or residual to the overall functioning of society. The social work profession attempts to work for social policies which do not condemn the social welfare institution to a status outside of the mainstream of society; i.e., one in which it does no more than pick up the pieces left behind by other institutions. In working for enlightened social policies and for the institutionalization of social welfare within the core social structure, the social work profession carries out one of its own key roles.

Social Policy: A Closer Look

The social work profession has a responsibility to the social welfare institution to help shape the development of social policy. Two basic questions, therefore, must be considered. What is social policy? How is it shaped? To paraphrase the definitions of Levy and Burns cited earlier in this paper, social policy is the system of value decisions guiding society or organized efforts used by society in acting on social needs or problems.[25] Social policy has been further conceptualized by Alfred Kahn as "the field of non-market benefits, entitlements, services, and transactions in this society--entitlements to rights and benefits by other than market criteria--or what an economist would call unilateral transfers."[26] It encompasses "the effort, by political action and social action, to guide and to control some aspects of the market by non-market criteria as well."[27] It also includes the policy analysis necessary to understand the consequences of different choices which inform those actions.[28] Kahn's conceptualization incorporates policy analysis and political and social action as intrinsic components of social policy, but does not address tha question of how social policy is actually shaped. A critique of the works of Richard Titmuss points to his neglect also of this aspect. David Reisman described Titmuss' view of social policy as concerned with "those needs which must be satisfied if the existing social matrix is to continue in existence" and "those states of dependency which are generally recognized by the collectivity to be collective responsibilities."[29] In discussing the development of social policies by society to meet its stabilizing needs and collective responsibilities, Reisman noted, however, that

> Titmuss chose to neglect the role of pressure groups in the decision-making process; for in

---

[25] See pp. 9-14 above for a fuller discussion of this question.

[26] Alfred J. Kahn, "1978 Alumni Conference Address: Social Policy," Columbia University School of Social Work <u>Alumni Newsletter</u>, Winter 1978-1979, p. 5.

[27] Ibid.

[28] Ibid.

[29] David A. Reisman, <u>Richard Titmuss: Welfare and Society</u> (London: Heinemann, 1977), p. 10.

> the real world the emergence of policies as an expression of values presupposes not only that people are able to recognize their interests and formulate their convictions . . . but also that they are powerful and militant enough to defend those interests and convictions through pressure from below.[30]

The question of how social policy is shaped is crucial to the ability of the social work profession to carry out meaningfully its function of leadership and guidance in the social welfare institution. Charles Lindblom's explanatory theory of the national policymaking process is that

> in the absence of universal agreement on what is to be done, someone has to either seize or be given "power" to decide. In actual fact, of course, "power" is always held by a number of persons rather than by one; hence policy is made through the complex processes by which these persons exert power or influence over each other.[31]

He defines as leaders in the policymaking process both the persons who are immediate participants in policy decisions (whom he calls proximate policy makers) and others

> who, though not proximate policy makers, exert significantly more influence on the proximate policy makers than do ordinary citizens and voters (for example, an interest-group leader, an influential editor or writer, or a party leader who does not enter the circle of proximate policy makers).[32]

---

[30] Ibid., p. 38.

[31] Lindblom, p. 29.

[32] Ibid., p. 30.

Robert Dahl's hierarchical conception of leaders, subleaders, and constituents is similar to Lindblom's groupings. Dahl notes that "many constituents have no direct influence at all; most people have very little. Subleaders of course have much more; the influence of the most powerful subleaders merges imperceptibly into that of leaders."[33]

Since the power to make policy is not vested in any single authority, the group just below or outside of the inner circle of proximate policy makers (Dahl's "subleaders") can have a hand in determining and shaping social policy through influencing the decisions of the proximate policy makers. The key to influencing those decisions, according to Lindblom, is persuasion, particularly through the skilled practice of partisan analysis, or "policy analysis by one policy maker to find a way in which a policy he desires can serve the values of another policy maker to whom the persuasion is directed."[34] Interest-group leaders and others close to proximate policy makers enhance the likelihood that their views will be heeded by the use of partisan analysis as a technique of persuasion.

Proximate policy makers in our society make the actual policy decisions; other leaders influence them. Operating within the theoretical framework which links profession to institution and mandates direction of the institution as a role for the profession, Eveline M. Burns used her position as a leader in the social work profession to attempt to influence, directly and indirectly, decisions of proximate policy makers bearing on the social welfare institution. This study documents that effort with respect to the development of social policies on old age retirement and provides a first-hand picture of the professional/institutional relationship as translated into actual practice by a major figure in

---

[33] Robert A. Dahl, Who Governs? Democracy and Power in an American City (New Haven: Yale University Press, 1961), pp. 163-164.

[34] Lindblom, p. 33.

the social work field.

Methodology

The study is a qualitative analysis of the income security writings and related career activities of Dr. Burns between the years 1935-1960 on the issue of old age retirement. It shows how she viewed the social policy issue of old age retirement and how she used professional associations to act on her concerns in order to try to influence the legislative action and development of policy on that issue during those years.

The method of qualitative content analysis used in this inquiry follows in the path of the dissertation research done by Norma Kolko Phillips (Yeshiva University, D.S.W. 1981) and is gratefully acknowledged by the author of the present study. Phillips pointed out Robert Merton's distinction, as found in Bernard Berelson's Content Analysis in Communication Research,

> between qualitative and quantitative analysis--one uses qualitative analysis where there is more interest in the total problem, such as the zeitgeist of a period, while quantitative analysis is aimed at particular components of problems."[35]

Qualitative analysis in the present study allows the author to demonstrate relationships among historical conditions/events, the introduction/passage of legislation in response to them, and the use by an individual of policy analysis and professional leadership roles as a way of advocating on behalf of specific legislation and policies.

---

35 Norma Kolko Phillips, "Social Work, Government, and Social Welfare: The Social Security Act" (D.S.W. dissertation, Wurzweiler School of Social Work, Yeshiva University, 1981), p. 21.

Also in keeping with Phillips, the present inquiry is historical in nature. Phillips' research traced the events culminating in the passage of the Social Security Act to arrive at an understanding of "the nature of the dynamic relationship between government and the profession of social work."[36] The present study concentrates on a specific Social Security Act issue, concern with old age retirement, to understand the relationship between the profession and the social welfare institution as manifested in the efforts of an esteemed professional to lead and guide in institutional development and change.

Historical research collects evidence, analyzes and synthesizes it to arrive at an understanding and interpretation of "a whole"; i.e., of a larger picture.[37] Use of the historical method in the present study informed the choice of topic as to both content and time. The income security area of old age retirement has been a constant theme in Dr. Burns' writings and lent itself to exploration in her career over a key quarter century. The policy issue, potential loss of income due to retirement or chronological age and the need/responsibility for compensating for such loss, was also the subject of major legislative actions over the twenty-five years. Qualitative analysis has been used within an historical framework to examine, against the backdrop of the *zeitgeist* of the period, the changes in old age retirement legislation over time and the relationship of those changes to the efforts of Dr. Burns, as reflected in her policy analyses and the other professional leadership activities which she undertook on the issue, to catalyze professional and public interest for the purpose of influencing the direction of policy change.

Both primary and secondary source materials have been incorporated into the present analysis. Stuart notes that primary sources include

---

[36] Ibid.

[37] Stuart, p. 327.

> a broad range of materials: diaries, letters, reminiscences, and other documents produced by the participants in an event; the laws, regulations, and records produced by organizations; and many others.[38]

The primary sources examined in the present study include Dr. Burns' personal reminiscences obtained in a series of interviews as well as the books and other materials written by her, relevant public laws passed by Congress between 1935 and 1960, and the records of professional associations and organizations in which she took an active leadership role. Using the available evidence from primary and secondary sources, the study analyzes and draws conclusions about what Dr. Burns believed needed to be done; how she worked to affect or, at least, to have an effect on policy change; and the results of those efforts.

Statement of Bias

There are two areas of bias which are relevant to this study and need to be recognized by the author. The first is a personal bias; the second, an ideological one.

Personally, I both knew and liked Dr. Burns, the subject of the study. I met her when she was employed as a Consultant Economist by my employer, the Community Service Society of New York. I therefore had the privilege of considering her as my colleague as well as my mentor and my friend. At a party given in her honor to mark her eightieth birthday, numerous social workers and other leaders in the social welfare community spoke admiringly of her and her outstanding contributions to the field of social policy analysis. I subsequently heard and read many more such comments over the years, leading me to the decision that the most significant contribution which I could make to professional

---

[38] Ibid., p. 323.

knowledge would be to start to document the work of this remarkable woman.

Dr. Burns submitted to hours of interviews as part of the research process. Further, her personal library was the source of some of the materials which I used in carrying out the study. I have attempted to distance myself and not allow personal considerations to color my reading of the materials or the objectivity of the analysis. I have also utilized numerous materials from other sources so that I would be informed of other, confirming or contradictory points of view about the area under examination, her policy analysis work in it, and her other related activities. Since readers in the field of policy analysis are also likely to have known her and/or to be familiar with her work, I believe that my interpretations and conclusions will be the subject of rigorous scrutiny and have thus made every effort to treat the evidence as though the subject of the study were unknown to me personally.

The second bias is one of values rather than feelings. The values I bring as baggage come out of a social work tradition. They include the belief that persons should "have access to the resources, services, and opportunities which they require" and belief that social policy and legislation can and should be used "to improve social conditions and to promote social justice."[39] These beliefs incline me to be empathetic to many of the legislative actions taken during 1935-1960 on issues such as old age retirement, to the views expressed in Dr. Burns' work, and to the activities which she undertook, quite apart from my personal fondness for her.

Readers of this study will of course be aware, as I am, that both my values and my personal knowledge of Dr. Burns influenced my choice of a research topic. The findings and conclusions, however, are based on or backed up by written materials and documented facts. No relevant materials were found and screened out and no ideas

---

[39] NASW Code of Ethics, sections VI:P: 2, 6.

were rejected a *priori*. To the extent that values are part of the baggage of every researcher, mine may have infused this study. I have tried to guard, however, against their influencing or determining its outcome.

Limitations of the Scope of the Inquiry

The study focuses solely on Dr. Burns' written works and professional activities related to the issue of old age retirement income security policy during the years 1935-1960. It examines them in terms of historical conditions and events during the period and compares them to the legislation enacted during the same time frame for purposes of understanding the nature of the role of a professional leader in inspiring and shaping institutional change. Biographical data are included in a discrete section to provide background material about Dr. Burns, her career and her professional associations, but the study is not a biography per se. Neither is it an evaluation of her actual impact on social policy change, although it attempts to show where and how her efforts may have had an influence. Rather, the inquiry is limited to an historical analysis conceptualizing Dr. Burns' approach to policy change. It shows her use of policy analysis and professional associations. It addresses the issue of how a skilled professional can focus the interest of the profession on legislation to change the institution in which it operates. That conceptualization of the development of old age retirement policies in the years 1935-1960 in terms of the role of the social work profession and one of its esteemed leaders--taking into consideration historical conditions, Social Security legislative changes and Burnsian policy analysis and advocacy for change--constitutes the framework for, and defines the boundaries of, the research study.

CHAPTER II

BIOGRAPHICAL DATA

Eveline M. Burns was born Eveline Mabel Richardson on March 16, 1900 in London, England.[1] She was the first and only child of Frederick and Eveline (Falkner) Richardson. The senior Eveline died of puerperal fever two weeks after childbirth. Frederick Richardson remarried after a year or so had passed; his second marriage subsequently produced a half-sister and two half-brothers for young Eveline.

The Richardson family was middle-class and conservative in its origins and lifestyle. Mr. Richardson, Dr. Burns' father, was in charge of the London sales office for the family's silversmith firm in Sheffield, England. The firm, "Cornwall Works," was owned by his father. It was expected that Dr. Burns' two half-brothers, Jack and Frederick, would also someday join that family firm. There was no such expectation for the girls, Eveline and Mary; middle-class girls in early twentieth-century England were not expected to pursue careers.

Within the Richardson household, little attention was paid to the kinds of issues which might spark or nourish a concern for social justice. The family was, in large part, both apolitical and nonreligious. It was not a highly intellectual environment. Dr. Burns was, in fact, the first member of her immediate family to attend a university. Neither was it a warm and happy household. The parents quarreled heavily after the first few years of marriage and Eveline grew up feeling closer to her father's sister, who had no children of her own, than to her own stepmother.

---

[1] All of the information in this chapter, unless otherwise noted, comes directly from Dr. Burns' personal papers and interviews with her.

Young Eveline attended Streatham Secondary School from 1913 to 1916. Upon completion of her studies there, she won a London County Council Tuition Scholarship and, at age sixteen, entered the London School of Economics and Political Science. She began as a day student, but the need of the civilian labor market for workers during World War I, when many young males were out of the work force due to military service, led her to change to an evening program in her second year at the university. She took a position in the Trades Board Division of the Ministry of Labour, dealing with minimum wage regulations. Despite the fact that she was attending school evenings while working in a government department during the day, she managed to be active in university activities as well as to compile an outstanding academic record. She graduated from the London School of Economics in 1920 with First Class Honours in Economics.

The years from 1916 to 1920 were mind-expanding ones for Eveline. The atmosphere at the London School of Economics was intellectual and was heavily oriented toward issues such as poverty and inequality. The School's academic community as a whole evinced a concern for the poor. Income distribution and related issues, far from being the province of a few isolated individuals, were part of everyone's thoughts and figured prominently in the academic life. Both the intellectual currents in general and the social concerns in particular were very different from anything that Eveline had experienced up until that time.

It was the intellectual climate at the London School of Economics, rather than the charisma or influence of any single professor, that started Eveline on her way to a lifelong personal interest and professional career in thinking, speaking, teaching and writing about issues of economic security. She was, however, particularly impressed by certain contemporary English thinkers, such as A.C. Pigou and Sidney and Beatrice Webb, for the ways in which they developed and used analytical material to understand and explain socioeconomic phenomena.[2] From Pigou's writings, she acquired a sense that it was important to justify to oneself how one spent one's life, and that studies in the field of economics could be used later to explain to people about issues which would affect them and the world. From the work of the Webbs, she learned how seemingly dull and routine official records could be used to shed light on pressing social and economic issues and on their place in the world.

The intellectual ferment of the London School of Economics meshed well with Eveline Richardson's natural, sympathetic inclinations. It allowed her to give reign to her emotional concerns as well as to make full use of her mental abilities. Apparently, it was a two-way fit. She joined the faculty at the London School of Economics in 1921 while continuing work on her doctoral dissertation. In 1926, Eveline M. Burns was awarded a doctorate in economics, winning the School's Adam Smith Medal for the outstanding thesis of the year with her dissertation on Wages and the State, in which she dealt with the question of how wages are set and the basis on on which employers set them. She also managed to fit a social life into her crowded schedule. In 1922, Eveline Richardson married the fellow student whom she had been dating since undergraduate days, Arthur R. Burns.

Dr. Burns came to the United States in 1926 on a two-year Laura Spelman Rockefeller Fellowship. These fellowships were given by the Laura Spelman Rockefeller Foundation to young scholars from different countries, who had done social science doctoral studies during wartime, and who had likely

---

[2] A.C. Pigou (1877-1959) was a British economist and professor who wrote about socioeconomic issues; his works include Wealth and Welfare and The Economics of Welfare. Sidney and Beatrice Webb (1859-1947 and 1858-1943, respectively) were social reformers and the founders of the London School of Economics; they lectured there on occasion during Eveline's years at the School.

had more limited exposure to colleagues and to a variety of ideas because of the events of World War I. The purpose was to allow them to meet, to broaden their sights, and to expand their own and each other's knowledge. Dr. Burns spent the time reading about different approaches to economics, visiting trade unions, and increasing her understanding of the people and ideas in the field. At the end of the two-year fellowship period, she and her husband remained in this country, becoming naturalized citizens and filling various academic and government posts over the years. She was a member of the Graduate Department of Economics at Columbia University from 1928 to 1942. During that time, she also worked for a period in Washington, D.C., in 1934, as a staff member of the Committee on Economic Security, the committee appointed by President Franklin D. Roosevelt to develop social security legislation. She was recruited for the Committee on Economic Security staff by Merideth Richard Givens, who was in charge of staff looking into work programs for the Committee and someone with whom she had previously collaborated in conjunction with consultant work in New York. The nature of the Columbia University faculty position allowed her to work in both capacities at the same time, teaching in New York and commuting to Washington, D.C. for part of the week to work for the Committee.

In 1942, Dr. Burns took a leave of absence from the Columbia University Economics Department and returned to government service as Chief of the Economic Security and Health Section of the National Resources Planning Board. This board was set up by President Franklin D. Roosevelt during World War II to carry out post-war planning, with the goal of developing better physical and social policies for a post-war America. Dr. Burns' labors at the National Resources Planning Board culminated in a major report, Security, Work and Relief Policies. The board, however, had little public support and was dissolved shortly after its reports were issued.

After the dissolution of the National Resources Planning Board, Dr. Burns worked for the National

Planning Association in Washington, D.C. and held a visiting professorship at Bryn Mawr College. She also did extensive lecturing around the country about the work which had been done by the National Resources Planning Board. In 1946, she returned to New York City as Professor of Social Work at the Columbia University School of Social Work, charged with the development of a doctoral program for that school. She also taught courses there, in particular on Social Security and the financing of social welfare. She remained on the faculty until her retirement in 1967.

During the period from 1946-1967, Dr. Burns' primary professional position was as a faculty member at the Columbia University School of Social Work. She also held visiting professorships and fellowships with other institutions. In 1950-1951, she was a visiting professor at Princeton University. During 1954-1955, she traveled in Europe on a Guggenheim Fellowship and also held a visiting professorship of research in the summer of 1955 at Manchester University, England. In 1958-1959, she was American Delegate to the International Conference on Social Work in Tokyo and Vice-Chairman of its Commission I, and she traveled extensively in the Orient and the Mid-East under the auspices of the State Department. After retiring from Columbia in 1967, she held professorships at New York University's Graduate School of Social Work and at Barnard College, was a Consultant Economist at the Community Service Society of New York, and finally retired from paid employment in 1981 at the age of eighty-one.

Throughout her professional career, Dr. Burns held numerous appointed and elected positions in professional organizations and associations. She also served frequently on task forces and advisory committees for the government and other institutions. Among her organizational associations were membership in the Consumers' League of New York, American Economic Association, National Conference on Social Welfare, American Public Welfare Association, and American Public Health Association. In the years covered in the present study (1935-1960), she served in the following leadership capacities:

Consumers' League of New York: Vice President, President (1935-1938)

American Economic Association: Executive Committee member, Vice President (1951-1954)

Federal Advisory Council on Employment Security: Chairman of various committees (1952-1970)

Secretary of Health, Education and Welfare Hobby's Advisory Committee on Coverage Extension of the Social Security Act: Committee member (1953-1954)

National Conference on Social Welfare: Secretary, First Vice-President, President (1955-1958)

American Public Welfare Association: Legislative Policy Committee member (1956-1968)

White House Conference on Children: Steering Committee member (1959-1960)

Dating from the 1960s, Dr. Burns held additional elected and appointed positions nationally with the American Public Health Association, the Federal Advisory Committee on Area Redevelopment (subsequently the National Committee on Regional Economic Development), the National Council of the American Association of University Professors, and the 1979 Federal Advisory Council on Social Security. Locally in the 1960s, she served on Mayor Lindsay's Commission on Delivery of Health Services in New York City and on various committees (Subcommittee on Social Policy for Health Care, Executive Committee) of the New York Academy of Medicine. She has also served during her professional career as a consultant to many government agencies, including the Social Security Administration, Treasury Department and Federal Reserve Board at the national level and the New York Departments of Labor and Social Welfare at the state level. She was, in 1961, Chairman of the Social Security Commissioner's Advisory Committee to evaluate the research program of the Social Security

Administration and, in 1962, Chairman of its follow-up Advisory Committee on Long-Range Research.

Dr. Burns has written prolifically throughout her career. In the period from 1935 to 1960, there are four major works which address old age retirement income security policies in America. These four works are: Toward Social Security (1936); the National Resources Planning Board Report, Security, Work and Relief Policies (1942); The American Social Security System (1949; 2nd edition, 1951); and Social Security and Public Policy (1956). A more comprehensive list of her publications is included in Appendix I.

Dr. Burns' professional contributions have been widely recognized by academicians and social workers generally. She is the recipient of numerous honorary degrees and other major professional awards. She holds honorary doctorates from Western College in Ohio (1962), Western Reserve University (1968), Adelphi University (1968), Columbia University (1969), and Rutgers University (1981). In 1967, she was elected an Honorary Fellow of the London School of Economics. She has received distinguished service awards from the National Conference on Social Welfare, the Institute for Socioeconomic Studies, the Columbia University School of Social Work, the American Association of University Women, and many civic organizations.

Dr. Burns' awards were the recognition of a long career of professional commitment and leadership. In the following section, I shall document her professional leadership in the specific policy area of old age retirement issues in the United States in the period from 1935-1960.

PART TWO

BURNSIAN LEADERSHIP ON OLD AGE RETIREMENT ISSUES IN THE UNITED STATES (1935-1960)

CHAPTER III

THE HISTORICAL *ZEITGEIST*: MAJOR SHIFTS IN ECONOMIC AND SOCIAL CONDITIONS AND THE POLITICAL CLIMATE

The previous part set the study itself into a context: its purpose, its focus and biographical information about Eveline M. Burns, the social welfare professional being considered in this study as a model of professional leadership. In this part, I will examine that leadership. The first two chapters in Part Two describe the historical *zeitgeist* of the period from 1935 to 1960 and trace the changes in Social Security old age retirement legislation over those years, looking particularly at changes in coverage, the earnings test, benefit levels and the use of general revenues. Part Two then goes on to examine in detail the professional leadership and activities of Dr. Burns with respect to those policy issues in the same years.

This chapter provides an historical perspective on the period covered by the study. It divides and examines the 1935-1960 study period into three parts to highlight the differing *zeitgeists* in each of those parts: the years in which the nation was coming out of the Depression, the World War II and post-war years, and the Eisenhower years.

Coming Out of the Depression

Franklin D. Roosevelt was elected as President of the United States in 1932 in the midst of the worst economic conditions that this country had ever known. The Depression of 1929 had had a devastating impact and

> the effects of the crisis were visible for all to see. In addition to the inability of the stock market to sustain a rally, banks were closing, industries were failing, and farms were

> going into bankruptcy. Corporate profits, farm income, and wage earnings all fell, and the need for money brought the meaning of economic standstill literally and painfully into almost every home.[1]

President Roosevelt took office in the face of an immediate need for action to ameliorate the prevailing conditions; the program which he set into action at that time is known as the New Deal.

Roosevelt presented in the New Deal a multi-faceted approach to a multi-faceted problem.

> The task that faced the New Deal was threefold in character. The immediate need was to save the thirteen million unemployed from privation and despair. Beyond this, the government must help to set the wheels of economic life in motion again. Finally, it was pledged to seek permanent cures, if possible, for the deep-seated evils that had produced the industrial breakdown. In other words, the administration's aims were relief, recovery and reform.[2]

Roosevelt approached this effort through a process of compromise.[3] He "sought at the outset to bring all economic groups, including the business group, into his program."[4] On the one hand, "he favored heavy taxes on the well-to-do, and he deemed a balanced

---

[1] June Axinn and Herman Levin, Social Welfare: A History of the American Response to Need, 2nd ed. (New York: Harper & Row, 1982), p. 179.

[2] Arthur Meier Schlesinger, Political and Social Growth of the American People, 1865-1940, 3rd ed. (New York: Macmillan, 1941), p. 533.

[3] Dexter Perkins, The New Age of Franklin Roosevelt, 1932-45 (Chicago: University of Chicago Press, 1957), p. 17.

[4] Ibid., p. 12.

budget less significant than the relief of the unemployed."[5] On the other hand, he at no time sought to destroy the economic foundations of American society or the capitalist system on which it was based.

> Because he steered this middle course he was constantly assailed by zealots to his left, who urged him to move faster and farther, and by zealots to his right, who feared he was plunging the country into communism and chaos.[6]

Overall and in general, however, "the New Deal represented the public opinion of the nation."[7]

Between 1933 and 1935, the New Deal brought into being a vast number of programs in pursuit of its goals of relief, recovery and reform. The programs for relief included the Federal Emergency Relief Administration, which was superseded by the Works Progress Administration; the Civil Works Administration; and the Civilian Conservation Corps.[8] Among the programs which focused on recovery were the Public Works Administration; the National Recovery Administration; the National Labor Board, which was superseded by the National Labor Relations Board; and the Agricultural Adjustment Act, which provided for setting up the Agricultural Adjustment Administration.[9] In terms of reform, the New Deal put in place the Federal Deposit Insurance Corporation; the Securities and Exchange Commission; the Tennessee Valley Authority; and, central to the

---

[5] Ibid., p. 8.

[6] Schlesinger, Political and Social Growth of the American People, p. 521.

[7] Perkins, p. 72.

[8] Schlesinger, Political and Social Growth of the American People, pp. 524-529.

[9] Ibid., pp. 529-545.

purposes of this study, the Social Security Act.[10]

Social insurance concerns were already part of the public and Congressional agendas by the time President Roosevelt actively took up the cause. The American Association for Old Age Security, under the leadership of Abraham Epstein, had developed a proposal

> that the government offer states grants-in-aid equal to a third of the sum spent for pensions. Senator Clarence C. Dill of Washington and Representative William P. Connery, Jr., of Massachusetts introduced a bill to this effect in 1932; and by 1934 the House had passed the bill and the Senate Pensions Committee had given it a favorable report.[11]

In addition, Senator Robert F. Wagner of New York and Representative David J. Lewis of Maryland had introduced a bill in February 1934 calling for a nationwide unemployment compensation program modelled after the plan in use in Wisconsin at that time. "By the spring of 1934, . . . both the Wagner-Lewis and the Dill-Connery bills had developed momentum. It was clear that if the administration did not take action soon its hand would be forced."[12] The action taken by Roosevelt was to appoint a five-member Committee on Economic Security in June 1934, whose charge was to "report to the President not later than December 1, 1934, its recommendations concerning proposals which in its judgment will promote greater economic security."[13] The Committee was made up of

---

[10] Ibid., pp. 545-553.

[11] Arthur M. Schlesinger, Jr., The Coming of the New Deal (Boston: Houghton Mifflin, 1959), p. 303.

[12] Ibid.

[13] Security, Work, and Relief Policies, Report of the Committee on Long-Range Work and Relief Policies to the National Resources Planning Board, Eveline M.

Frances Perkins, Roosevelt's Secretary of Labor, as its chairman; Harry Hopkins, the administrator of the Federal Emergency Relief Administration; the Attorney General; and the federal Secretaries of Agriculture and Treasury.[14]

> The report of the Committee on Economic Security, transmitted to Congress by the President in the special message of January 17, 1935, made far-reaching proposals for the enactment of a Nation-wide program of old-age insurance, for the development of a Federal-State system of unemployment compensation, and for Federal grants-in-aid to the States for assistance to the aged and to dependent children and for certain health and welfare services. The Economic (later Social) Security Bill embodying these recommendations was introduced at that time and as modified became law on August 14, almost seven months later.[15]

In the seven months between the introduction of the Social Security legislation in Congress and its eventual enactment, there was heavy public clamor and controversy from its supporters, its opponents, and those who had their own proposals to offer as substitutes for one or another of its provisions. Support for the legislation came from

> such organizations as . . . [the] American Association for Labor Legislation, Abraham Epstein's American Association for Social Security, . . . church, consumer, and women's groups, and above all . . . the work on its

---

Burns, Director of Research (Washington, D.C.: Government Printing Office, 1942), p. 32.

14 Jacob Fisher, The Response of Social Work to the Depression (Cambridge, Mass.: Schenkman Publishing Co., 1980), p. 63.

15 Burns, Security, Work, and Relief Policies, p. 33.

behalf by organized labor.[16]

Opponents of the legislation were numerous, even though the social insurance portions had been crafted to take into account the probable objections of the Supreme Court, the medical profession, and organized farmers.[17]

> While the friends of social security were arguing out the details of the program, other Americans were regarding the whole idea with consternation, if not with horror. Organized business had long warned against such pernicious notions,

and the witnesses appearing before House and Senate committees to express opposition to the bill included spokesmen from the National Industrial Conference Board, the National Association of Manufacturers, General Motors, and the Chamber of Commerce.[18] Finally, pressuring for their own plan, were the Townsendites, Dr. Francis E. Townsend and his growing army of supporters.

> Above all, Congress worried about satisfying the great political pressure from advocates of the so-called Townsend plan, which would have required the government to give everyone over sixty pensions of $200 per month, provided they stopped gainful work and spent the momey within one month inside the United States. Old people joined Townsend's crusade in droves.[19]

---

[16] Fisher, p. 237.

[17] James T. Patterson, America's Struggle Against Poverty, 1900-1980 (Cambridge, Mass.: Harvard University Press, 1981), p. 75.

[18] Schlesinger, The Coming of the New Deal, p. 311.

[19] Patterson, pp. 70-71.

The supporters of the Social Security bill carried the day. Opposition in the House and Senate each collapsed before the respective votes were taken. The House passed the bill, albeit in a somewhat revised version, on April 19, 1935 by a vote of 371 to 33; the Senate passed its bill on the following June 19 by a vote of 76 to 6.[20] The two versions were then reconciled and, as stated above, the Social Security Act became law on August 14, 1935. A three-member Social Security Board was appointed in that same month to administer the act.[21] Its chairman was John Gilbert Winant, a former governor of New Hampshire; the other two members were Arthur Altmeyer and an Arkansas lawyer named Vincent Myles.[22]

The constitutionality of the Social Security Act was not immediately challenged in the Supreme Court; as discussed below, it did not meet a substantial challenge until 1937. Other of the New Deal measures, on the other hand, did come up in 1935-1936 for Supreme Court review. In 1935 and 1936, the Court invalidated a number of New Deal actions, including the National Industrial Recovery Administration and the Agricultural Adjustment Act.[23] By that time, however, "a considerable degree of recovery from the trough of the depression already had been achieved."[24] By the middle of 1936, industrial production, factory employment, farm prices, and the national income were all up and unemployment had shrunk considerably; overall, 1936

---

[20] Schlesinger, The Coming of the New Deal, p. 312.

[21] Burns, Security, Work, and Relief Policies, p. 33.

[22] Schlesinger, The Coming of the New Deal, pp. 312-313.

[23] Perkins, pp. 43-44.

[24] Burns, Security, Work, and Relief Policies, p. 22.

was "a year of very substantial economic recovery."[25] It was, in fact, "the high point of the recovery under the New Deal."[26] It was also a presidential election year.

> The forthcoming election of 1936
>
> afforded a natural occasion for the electorate to take general stock of the "Roosevelt revolution." . . . Though people differed violently in opinion, the vast majority, as the outcome of the election was to show, viewed the results with high approval.[27]

Those violent differences of opinion, however, had earlier given rise to organized pressure groups on both the left and the right which were to play a role in the 1936 election.

> Of the various groups urging more radical action, each possessed its own panacea, carried on a colorful agitation and optimistically claimed millions of followers. The Share-Our-Wealth Society, captained by Senator Huey P. Long, political dictator of Louisiana, demanded a redistribution of wealth so that every family should have at least five thousand dollars and none possess more than three or four million. When Long was assassinated by a foe in his state in September, 1935, the mantle of his leadership fell on the Reverend Gerald L. K. Smith. Another organization, comprising six thousand local clubs, espoused the proposal of Dr. Francis E. Townsend, a sexagenarian California physician who had lost his savings in the depression. This plan called on the federal government to pay monthly pensions of two

---

[25] Perkins, p. 51.

[26] Ibid., p. 56.

[27] Schlesinger, Political and Social Growth of the American People, p. 555.

hundred dollars to all needy unemployed persons over sixty years of age who should agree to spend the money as rapidly as they received it. By this means it was hoped to stimulate business and at the same time make ampler provision for the aged. Of the other pressure groups the most important was the National Union for Social Justice, founded in 1935 by the Reverend Charles E. Coughlin of Detroit, a Catholic priest who had built up a vast radio following through his emphatic utterances on public affairs. At first a supporter of Roosevelt, he later came to class him with bankers and brokers as obstructing the true path to progress. Father Coughlin's organization advocated a somewhat vague program which centered in the demand that the government should own all the banks and natural resources and alone exercise the power to create currency and credit.

To the extreme right of these groups stood the American Liberty League, formed in 1934 to "combat radicalism, preserve property rights and uphold and preserve the Constitution."[28]

The 1936 presidential election became a contest between Franklin D. Roosevelt, the Democratic incumbent responsible for the New Deal; Republican Alfred M. Landon, a former governor of Kansas; and Congressman William Lemke of North Dakota, the candidate of a new, minor political party, the Union Party. The latter was, according to one observer, "a hastily put together coalition of radical rightists like the radio priest Father Coughlin and Gerald L. K. Smith; of populists distrustful of Roosevelt; and of such one-issue crusaders as Dr. Townsend."[29] The American Liberty League came into the picture on the

---

[28] Ibid., pp. 560-561.

[29] Fisher, p. 140. The "radical rightists" term is his; others may have viewed those political philosophies differently.

side of the Republican ticket.[30] By the time the campaign ended, however, overall public sentiment with regard to Roosevelt's policies was clear.

> Despite the din and confusion of the contest, the result stood at no time in serious doubt. . . . Roosevelt swept every state but Maine and Vermont, winning 523 electoral votes to 8 for Landon and 60.7 per cent of the popular ballots (27,750,000 votes) to 36.4 per cent (16,680,000) for his rival.[31]

Lemke received less than a million votes.[32]

Early in Roosevelt's second term, the Social Security Act faced a critical test as it became yet another of the New Deal programs to be challenged in the Supreme Court. At issue was whether the Act's provisions for the levying of taxes and payment of benefits for old age retirement fell within Congress' right to spend money in aid of the general welfare. In May 1937, in Helvering v. Davis, the Court determined that Congress had indeed been within its rights in setting up such a nationwide program for general welfare purposes. "When money is spent to promote the general welfare, the concept of welfare or the opposite is shaped by Congress, not the states. So the concept be not arbitrary, the locality must yield."[33] The Court's acceptance of Congressional power to establish this nationwide program of taxation and benefits to promote the general welfare of the populace not only helped generally in terms of solidifying the New Deal, but

---

[30] Schlesinger, Political and Social Growth of the American People, p. 565.

[31] Ibid., pp. 565-566.

[32] Fisher, p. 140.

[33] Helvering v. Davis, 301 U.S. 671, 57 Sup. Ct. 792, 81 L.Ed. 1336 (1937), reproduced in Phillips, pp. 325-332.

also provided the base from which further Social Security legislation could proceed in the years ahead.

Midway into Roosevelt's second term, the national economy took one last, unexpected downturn as part of its emergence from the Depression period. A business slump which began in 1937 turned into a recession in 1938,

> with falling industrial activity, lagging retail business, declining stock markets and rising unemployment. The major cause was probably the government's sharp retrenchment of expenditures during the period of reviving prosperity in 1936-1937 or, to turn the proposition around, the failure of private business to expand as rapidly as the federal outlays shrank.[34]

Roosevelt quickly ordered the resumption of federal action to pump money back into the economy. The recession was worrisome, but it was short-lived. "Nearly all business indicators were up in '39, and by the end of that year were pointing to another surge in the economy."[35] That was fortunate, also, because by then other issues were commanding Roosevelt's attention; the United States was moving toward World War II.

The World War II and Post-War Years

The 1940s brought marked change to the American society. For one thing, they brought prosperity and real economic progress. With regard to economic conditions generally,

> there was no doubting that absolute poverty diminished rapidly between 1939 and 1941,

---

[34] Schlesinger, Political and Social Growth of the American People, p. 579.

[35] Fisher, p. 176.

> continued to fall during World War II, and decreased, though much less rapidly, from 1946 to 1956. The key to this progress was not welfare, which was relatively insignificant, but economic growth,

emanating in large part from the heavy government spending during World War II.[36] Between 1940 and 1945, the gross national product rose by 56 percent in real terms--that is, after adjusting for the effect of inflation.[37] Not only did income rise in the 1940s for families in all income ranges, "but it rose proportionately more for poor families than for rich ones."[38] The war years brought increased economic opportunities to women and blacks; in the latter case, however, it did not happen without a struggle. "The wartime redistribution of jobs and income was not achieved easily. Tremendous resistance to the employment of blacks in defense industries was encountered, and race riots occurred in 1940 and 1941."[39]

With domestic prosperity on the rise and family life on the decline as a result of World War II, the social legislation of that era shifted concomitantly from economic to other issues.

> The social legislation of the time was primarily related to the needs of communities disrupted by army camps and war plants and to the needs of families dislocated by the absence of husbands and fathers as they left for the armed forces or for war industries and by the absence of mothers as women took jobs. Housing, day care, education, health, recreation and transportation needs as they affected "home front" preparations

---

[36] Patterson, pp. 79-80.

[37] Axinn and Levin, p. 237.

[38] Ibid.

[39] Ibid., p. 238.

became the focus of concern.[40]

Despite the improved economic conditions which allowed legislative attention to focus on other areas of concern during the war, however, the prosperity was not universal. In 1942, the National Resources Planning Board issued a report, authored by Eveline M. Burns, which set forth the continuing income needs of the population for post-war planning purposes.

> Though the NRPB actually underestimated the extent of need, its report was in every way a far-seeing document. It called in effect for a federally supported floor under income. President Roosevelt waited sixteen months before forwarding the report to Congress, but he ultimately reflected the NRPB's point of view in his Economic Bill of Rights of January 1944. All citizens, he said, deserved useful and remunerative jobs; income to provide sufficient food, clothing, and recreation; decent lodgings; medical care; protection against the hazards of old age, sickness, accident, and unemployment; and a good education.[41]

The nation was already giving thought to the post-war years. When they came, they were influenced not only by the changed economic conditions, but also by two other major changes which had taken place during the war years. These were a large-scale movement of population, which had converted the nation from a rural into an urban society, and a new sense of mobility, which had grown out of the increased ease of transportation and communication.[42] Both of these trends had been fostered to meet wartime needs; both of them, as well as the war-induced prosperity, would have an impact on American society and social attitudes in the following decade.

---

[40] Ibid., p. 241.

[41] Patterson, pp. 92-93.

[42] Axinn and Levin, pp. 234-235.

The Eisenhower Years

The election of General Dwight D. Eisenhower to the Presidency of the United States in 1952 was a legacy of the war years. So, too, were several of the important economic and social conditions prevailing at that time. For one thing, the nation was not only at peace, but was prosperous. Government money was being pumped into the domestic economy through the provisions of the Servicemen's Readjustment Act of 1944, more popularly known as the G.I. Bill, and the Social Security Act of 1935.

> Even more important was the enormous backlog of demand for major consumer goods that had been unavailable during the war--new housing and automobiles, for example. The postwar spurt in marriages and births added to market demand for goods. The combination of needs and wartime savings stimulated the expansion of older industries and the development of such new products as television.[43]

A new faith in the nation's economic system had taken root, and "by the mid-1950s younger Americans who had not been adults during the Depression began to take prosperity for granted."[44]

Poverty and need continued to exist in the 1950s, as the National Resources Planning Board report had predicted, but both the locus and composition of that poverty were markedly different from what they had been before the war. As the general population had moved from rural to urban areas, poverty, too, had moved. It had shifted to the North and the cities. "By 1960 some 55 percent of the poor lived in cities, 30 percent in small towns, and only 15 percent on farms, as opposed to

---

[43] Ibid., p. 244.

[44] Patterson, p. 85.

around 50 percent in the mid 1930s who had done some farming."[45] Poverty had also shifted from being a problem of the general populace to being a problem primarily of small farmers, the aged, non-whites and members of broken families.[46] Of those groups, it was the aged who elicited the broadest public sentiment and concern. They were growing in number, the rural-to-urban shift meant they would not fit so easily into the economic and family structure as previously, and the increased mobility of American workers was perceived as having an adverse effect upon reliance on the family as the basic source of an individual's economic security.[47] Given the public's concern in the 1950s for Social Security over public welfare, Congress "took the simple way out by liberalizing social insurance and maintaining a policy of benign neglect toward welfare."[48] Congressional legislation in the 1950s "quietly added millions of workers to the OASI system."[49]

The 1950s were not entirely devoid of frustration for the general American public. For one thing, the Korean War in which we engaged during those years ended in a stalemate.[50] The decade also included a period of political repression which began as a result of Senator Joseph McCarthy's "witchhunt against those who had been 'soft on communism'" and did not subside until the Senate censured his tactics in 1954.[51] In general, however, the 1950s were

---

[45] Ibid., p. 80.

[46] Ibid., pp. 80-81.

[47] Eveline M. Burns, The American Social Security System, 2nd ed. (Boston: Houghton Mifflin, The Riverside Press, 1951), pp. 25-26.

[48] Patterson, p. 90.

[49] Ibid., p. 94.

[50] Axinn and Levin, p. 245.

[51] Ibid.

years of affluence and consumerism. They represented a decade "of overall self-satisfaction" on the part of the American public.[52]

Findings

The period from 1935 to 1960 in the United States was characterized by several distinct shifts in economic and social conditions and political climate. The earliest part of that period was spent coming out of the Depression. That was followed by World War II and the post-war years, which were in turn followed by the Eisenhower years of the 1950s.

The climb out of the Depression was long and difficult. It was engineered by President Franklin D. Roosevelt through his New Deal. The programs of that era, which included the Social Security Act, were, in some cases, highly controversial. The general trend of public sentiment, however, was on his side, despite attacks from both the left and the right. The New Deal programs set the nation back on a desirable economic course and Roosevelt won reelection by a landslide in 1936. Shortly thereafter, the constitutionality of the Social Security Act was challenged. The Act was sustained, however, by the Supreme Court in May 1937, marking a victory for New Deal social legislation and paving the way for the future growth of Social Security. As for the nation's economy, there was another, temporary slump in 1937 and 1938, but by the following year it was once again on an upward path.

The war years brought economic prosperity, with jobs and rising income for many people. The needs and demands of those years gave new economic opportunities to women and blacks. Legislative concerns turned from economic security to the needs of communities and families upset or split apart by the war. Two important trends which developed during

---

[52] Ibid.

the war years and which had an impact on the post-war period were the migration of the population from rural to urban areas and a heightened sense of mobility on the part of the general populace. Finally, the lasting prosperity of the post-war years renewed public faith in the American economic system.

The Eisenhower years were primarily years of self-satisfaction on the part of the American public. Poverty was now found more in the cities than elsewhere and the poverty population was, by now, mostly an amalgam of disadvantaged groups: small farmers, the aged, non-whites and members of broken families. Concern for the aged led to considerable liberalizations of the Social Security program in the 1950s, but public welfare was for the most part ignored during those years.

This chapter has described the historical *zeitgeist* of the years from 1935 to 1960. In the following chapter, I will examine the Social Security old age retirement legislation which was enacted in those years. The study will trace the changes made over the twenty-five year period which began with the passage of the Social Security Act in 1935.

CHAPTER IV

LEGISLATION RELATING TO RETIREMENT OR CHRONOLOGICAL AGE

In the previous chapter, the study examined the evolving social and political climate of the years 1935-1960. It found that the apparent need for and acceptance of differing degrees of social legislation appeared to vary as social and political conditions in the country themselves varied. This chapter will examine the social policy issue of old age retirement income security and the specific federal legislation which was enacted in that public policy area during the twenty-five years under study.

Circumstances Resulting in Loss of Income

Retirement from the labor force results in a loss of individual and household income for workers and their dependents. It has been noted that, "prior to retirement, earnings constitute about 87 percent of the aggregate money income for the entire population."[1] After retirement, most or all of that income is no longer available.

> Since earnings from work constitute the primary source of income for most individuals, the cessation of these earnings upon retirement imposes an economic hardship for most elderly which society has sought to ameliorate through a variety of public and private programs.[2]

The reasons for entering retirement, which are

---

[1] Gary Nelson, "Social Class and Public Policy for the Elderly," Social Service Review 56 (March 1982): 86.

[2] Ibid., p. 89.

not mutually exclusive, include a voluntary decision to leave employment upon reaching a specified pensionable or chronological age, an employment requirement that an individual stop working at a given job at a specified point in time, deteriorating health which may make the individual unable or unwilling to work, and loss of a job in later years and inability to find a suitable new one.[3]

The Social Security Act retirement legislation enacted in 1935 made provision to pay benefits, beginning in 1942, to eligible retired workers age sixty-five and over in order to replace a portion of the income lost as a consequence of retirement and thereby help to prevent impoverishment in old age. In the years 1935-1960, there were changes enacted in that retirement legislation in terms of the occupational categories covered, the mechanism for computing the benefit amounts, the allowable earnings for retirees' benefit eligibility, the types of monthly benefits available, the contribution rates for workers and employers, and the use of general revenues for Social Security program purposes. Each of these types of program change and its relationship to the overall Social Security retirement program is discussed in the next section.

The Evolving Legislation: Title II of the Social Security Act

---

[3] The 1979 Advisory Council on Social Security noted in a discussion of early retirement that workers who claim Social Security benefits before age sixty-five generally do so because of ill health or inability to find suitable work after a job loss, or because they prefer leisure to work, may already have a retired spouse, and are assured of income through Social Security and, often, private pensions and savings. See: Advisory Council on Social Security, Social Security Financing and Benefits, p. 165.

When the Social Security Act was passed in 1935, it established a system for the payment of old age benefits covering workers in commerce and industry (excluding railroad workers).[4] It did not cover farm or domestic workers, self-employed individuals, members of the uniformed services or religious orders, government employees, or employees of nonprofit organizations. Benefits were to be computed based on total wages in covered employment, up to $3,000 annually, received after December 31, 1936 and prior to age sixty-five. The monthly benefit computation formula was 1/2 percent of the first $3,000 of total countable wages plus 1/12 percent of the next $42,000 plus 1/24 percent of total countable wages over $45,000. No earnings were allowed to beneficiaries; the law decreed that the total monthly benefit be withheld from an otherwise qualified individual in each month in which he received wages from employment.[5] Benefits were to be available only to workers at least sixty-five years of age who had received at least $2,000 in total wages between December 31, 1936 and the attainment of age sixty-five and who had received those wages on some day of at least five different years in that same time period. They were to be payable beginning in 1942. The money for payment of benefits was to be

---

[4] Historical details of the legislation and its chronological changes are found in Phillips, Social Work, Government, and Social Welfare; Martha Derthick, Policymaking for Social Security (Washington, D.C.: Brookings Institution, 1979); Eveline M. Burns, Toward Social Security: An Explanation of the Social Security Act and a Survey of the Larger Issues (New York: McGraw-Hill, 1936); and the Social Security Bulletin, Annual Statistical Supplement.

[5] This provision had a double purpose. In addition to insuring that the beneficiary had actually retired, the requirement for total withdrawal from paid employment was meant to open up labor market opportunities for younger workers at a time when jobs were scarce and unemployment was high.

collected through a wage and payroll tax earmarked specifically for Social Security purposes. The contribution rate was set at 1 percent each for employees and employers, to be paid on annual wages up to $3,000. The tax was scheduled to be imposed as of January 1, 1937 and to rise in steps to 3 percent each on employees and employers by 1949. Although the legislative intent was clearly that the program should be self-sufficient and that the contributions made through the wage and payroll tax should pay for the program costs, provision was made in the 1935 legislation for an appropriation from general revenues in the event that actuarial estimates were inaccurate. If the collections from the wage and payroll tax were insufficient to cover the costs of current benefits plus administration plus an old age reserve to meet the claims of contributors, the 1935 Act provided for the difference to be made up through general tax revenues.

Changes in the original Social Security Act provisions were enacted starting in 1939 and other changes came frequently thereafter.

Extensions of Coverage

In 1935, Social Security coverage was compulsory for, and limited to, workers in commerce and industry (except railroads) under age sixty-five. In 1939, it was expanded to include workers in those categories aged sixty-five and over. In 1950, compulsory coverage was mandated for some categories of regularly employed farm and domestic workers, nonfarm self-employed other than members of professional groups, federal civilian employees not under a federal retirement system, and certain workers outside of the United States. In 1951, railroad workers with less than ten years of service were folded into the Social Security system. In 1954, more categories of farm, domestic and self-employed workers were required to join the Social Security system. The remainder of the professional self-employed, except physicians, were added in 1956, as were members of the uniformed services. In 1960, additional out-of-the-country workers and parents working for their children were mandatorily brought under the system.

In addition to expanding the occupational groups for which Social Security coverage was mandatory, changes in the legislation began to allow for elective coverage beginning in 1950. In that year, state and local government employees not under a state or local government retirement system and employees (other than ministers) of nonprofit organizations were permitted to join the Social Security system. In 1954 and 1956, elective coverage was further extended; the system was made available to additional groups of state and local government employees and to ministers.

Other Liberalizations

In addition to its extension of the Social Security system to cover more and more workers, the Social Security legislation enacted after 1935 liberalized the program in a number of other ways. The benefit computation formula was modified legislatively five times between 1935 and 1960 and current benefit levels were increased, leading to higher benefit levels for all beneficiaries. The earnings test, the test of whether a claimant is entitled to retirement benefits, was changed in those years both in the amount of allowable earnings and in the ages at which it applies. Originally allowing for no earnings for any beneficiary, the amount of allowable earnings without loss of the monthly benefit was increased in 1939, 1950, 1952, 1954, and 1958. The 1950 legislation also exempted beneficiaries aged seventy-five and older from the earnings test altogether. This meant that people age seventy-five and up could collect their Social Security benefits regardless of the amount of income earned. In 1954, the age of exemption from the earnings test was lowered to seventy-two years.

Another important area of legislative change, in terms of the growth of Social Security, was that new categories of monthly benefits were added subsequent to the original legislation. The 1935 Act provided for benefits to workers only. In 1939, legislation provided for the first time for dependents' benefits. Benefit eligibility on the record of a retired worker was made available to wives age sixty-five and older and to children up to age sixteen or, in the case of students, up to age eighteen. The requirement that sixteen- and seventeen-year-old children be students in order to be eligible for benefits as dependents of a retired worker was eliminated in 1946. In 1950, the provisions governing wives' benefits were liberalized to allow the wife of a retired worker to collect monthly benefits before the age of sixty-five if she was caring for a child who was eligible for benefits. As long as she had an eligible child in her care, she could collect benefits regardless of her age. The 1950 legislation also provided, for the first time, that benefits could be payable to a dependent husband, age sixty-five or over, of a retired insured female worker. Previously, wives' benefits were available based on their husbands' work records, but men could not draw benefits based on their wives' work. The 1950 legislation did not provide men with automatic entitlement to spouse benefits upon attainment of a specified age, which would have been the equivalent of the existing wives' benefits. It did, however, recognize and provide benefits for a new, albeit limited, category of dependents: husbands who had been dependent upon a wife's earnings and who thereby suffered a loss of income support upon her retirement.

Further liberalizations with respect to eligibility for benefits were enacted in 1956. An eligible female worker or wife of a retired male worker could, by virtue of the 1956 legislation, collect actuarially reduced benefits beginning as early as age sixty-two. Previously, the minimum age at which one or the other could have collected benefits would have been sixty-five years, except for younger wives of retired workers who had eligible dependent children in their care. Also in 1956, provisions governing children's benefits for disabled children of retired workers were liberalized, allowing them to continue even after the child attained eighteen years of age, so long as the disability existed prior to age eighteen.

Financing Changes

There were multiple extensions of coverage and program liberalizations which took place in Social Security over the program's first quarter of a century. There were also changes in program financing over those years. Social Security benefits are financed through special wage and payroll taxes which are levied equally on employees and employers. The tax is equal to a specified percent of a person's salary, up to a maximum amount. The first Social Security taxes were scheduled in the 1935 legislation for collection beginning in 1937. An employee and his employer were each responsible for a tax payment equal to 1 percent of the person's salary, up to a maximum salary amount of $3,000 per year. The percent to be paid, or contribution rate, was raised four times between 1935 and 1960, from 1 percent each for an employee and his employer at the outset to 1.5 percent each in 1950, 2 percent each in 1954, 2.25 percent each in 1959 and 2.75 percent each in 1960. The amount of annual salary on which these percentages had to be paid, called the earnings base, was also increased over the years. The original earnings base of $3,000 rose to $3,600 in 1951, $4,200 in 1955, and $4,800 in 1959. The maximum annual Social Security contribution on a worker's earnings went from $30 each by an employee and employer in 1937 to $132 each in 1960.

Contributions to the Social Security program grew, therefore, in three ways: through an increased number of contributors brought into the program under newly extended coverage provisions, through increases in the contribution rate, and through increases in the earnings base. These contributions were sufficient to finance the program, in terms of both benefit outlays and administrative costs, on a pay-as-you-go basis from year to year.

The other potential funding source which has been considered for Social Security, apart from the wage and payroll taxes, has been general revenues. The use of general tax revenues, if necessary, was made a part of the 1935 legislation. In 1939, the Social Security trust fund was created from which benefits and administrative expenses were to be paid. Legislation passed in 1944 again authorized the use of general revenues, if necessary, to make up any deficit in the financing of the Social Security program. That general authorization was repealed in 1950.

Title II of the Social Security Act, the underpinning of the entire Social Security program of old age benefits, continued to evolve legislatively after its genesis in 1935 to include more workers, to expand eligibility, to provide larger basic benefits, to provide additional types of benefits, and to help keep the program income in step with program outlays.

Policy Alternatives

In its first quarter century, the Social Security program moved toward liberalizing and broadening the scope of the program. This growth was sporadic, but it was steady. Each of the changes was the result of legislation, which must be passed by both Houses of Congress and signed by the President in order to take effect. The policy alternatives would have been to make no major legislative changes in Social Security old age provisions or to change the program by restricting, rather than enlarging, it.

The number of people covered under Social Security would have increased as the program matured even without additional legislation. As more workers in covered employment earned sufficient quarters of coverage to be insured for benefits, program numbers would have increased in any event. However, the new laws brought additional occupational groups into the program, thereby expanding coverage far beyond the growth which would have ensued naturally from the 1935 legislation. The natural program maturing and the expanded coverage together increased protection dramatically. In 1950, fifteen years after enactment, about a fourth of all older people were protected by Social Security. By 1960, that number had risen to over 70 percent.[6] In addition to the legislative extension of coverage to new groups of workers, the changes after 1935 extended benefits to new groups of dependents. Had the Congress and the public not wanted to see the Social Security program expanded, these changes need not have been made. It might also have been thought desirable to bring in additional occupational groups, both for the current revenues to the program and for prevention of future penury for workers in those groups, without the enactment of dependents' benefits. That, too, did not happen.

Likewise, there was no pressing need to liberalize either the earnings test or the manner in which benefits were computed so as to provide for larger benefits or benefits to a few more people. It is not difficult to envision a scenario in which a complex benefit formula remains relatively constant, especially since legislated increases in the tax rate and the earnings base affect more people at the time of enactment than benefit from a revised formula. For the working population, which is far larger than the retired population, the additional Social Security taxes are felt immediately; the gains are to be realized only in the future. Derthick attributes the policymaking decisions and results which allowed, indeed forced, an expansionary program to a combination of program complexity and expert, liberalminded administrators and allies.

---

[6] Robert M. Ball, Social Security Today and Tomorrow (New York: Columbia University Press, 1978), p. 14.

> Combined with its extreme technicality, compromise and ambiguity helped to render the program incomprehensible to all but a highly expert few at the proprietary core of policymaking, and it helped these few to reach compromises among themselves and to manipulate public presentation of the program in a way that would facilitate acceptance.[7]

To Ball, one of Derthick's "expert few at the proprietary core of policymaking," there is no wondering at the fact that Social Security has been a highly regarded program and that therefore the policies of liberalization have been widely accepted over the years.

> Because they are payable as an earned right, the benefits accord with the self-respect of people accustomed to providing for themselves. It is small wonder that the Congress and the people have preferred contributory social insurance to a system benefiting only those who can show themselves to be destitute.[8]

Not all of the expert analysts have taken such a sanguine view of the inevitability of program acceptance. Myers notes that political philosophies have played an important role in Social Security policymaking over the years.[9] He views policy alternatives as emerging out of a philosophy of what

---

[7] Derthick, p. 291.

[8] Ball, pp. 486-487. Robert M. Ball was one of the top-level program executives in the Social Security Administration for many years; he eventually became the Social Security Commissioner, holding that post from 1962 to 1973.

[9] Robert J. Myers, Social Security, 2nd ed. (Bryn Mawr, Pa.: McCahan Foundation, 1981), p. 167. Robert J. Myers was associated with the Social Security Administration from its inception and was its chief actuary from 1947 to 1970.

role a Social Security program should play in a nation's economic and social life. According to Myers, there are three broad philosophies: laissez-faire, in which there would be no Social Security program and people would be expected, for the most part, to take care of themselves; expansionist, in which full economic security for those who no longer have earnings would be provided by government programs; and moderate, in which government social insurance programs such as Social Security and the private sector play complementary roles in providing for economic security.[10] While the laissez-faire and expansionist philosophies presented by Myers are extreme, they are nevertheless real and each has and has had its adherents over the years. Within the moderate viewpoint itself, there clearly has been the possibility of a broad range of policy alternatives, from a mix consisting of more government and less private sector involvement to just the opposite.

The role played by active public advocacy, as contrasted to simple public acceptance, of liberalizations in Social Security retirement programs has been difficult to distinguish. Derthick points out the manipulation and cooptation of public participation, including both the relatively informed as well as lay public groups and individuals. Program executives had in mind their policy goals for the Social Security program and paid close attention to the grooming of the public and Congressional leaders necessary for movement toward those goals. They set out preferred policy changes incrementally, worked at anticipating and shaping general public reaction, brought business and labor leaders to their side to assist with their agenda, and worked closely with the relevant Congressional leadership. Although the representatives of any or all of these interest groups--the general public, business, labor, or Congress--could theoretically have developed a different conception of the program and pursued a different set of policies, the experts had clearly mastered leadership as well as technical details.

---

[10] Ibid., pp. 327-330.

> Policymaking came to resemble a prolonged symphony in which the movements were conceived by the executive "composers." There were no intermissions except that caused by World War II. . . . The congressional committees responded in their own fashion, rejecting now, accepting later, and selecting to suit their collective preferences and the preferences of the whole legislature, pertinent interest groups, and the public as the committees perceived them.[11]

The shape of those preferences, however, had not been left to chance. Business, labor and lay leaders were invited to participate on Social Security advisory councils, where they could be exposed to and influenced by the program executives' policy perspectives. Likewise, general public opinion was treated with great seriousness and concern.

> One of the most conspicuous features of policymaking for social security is the preoccupation of policymakers with public psychology. They have been enormously concerned with the public's perceptions and subjective experience of the program. . . . The influence of public opinion on the program, though real, is manifested indirectly, in actions of the policymakers that anticipate public reaction and respond to what they believe the public prefers; and even then influence runs in both directions. Policymakers have presented the program so as to induce a favorable mass response.[12]

In terms of policy alternatives to the Social Security retirement program, perhaps the single largest threat was not to one or another of the incremental changes introduced after enactment of the program in 1935, but to the enactment of that program itself. An alternative program for old age economic security had been proposed and had gained numerous

---

[11] Derthick, pp. 46-47.

[12] Ibid., p. 183.

adherents in the early 1930s. Dr. Francis E. Townsend, a physician, had developed a plan to give $200 per month to everyone over sixty years of age, a platform which served as the basis for organizing a growing national network of Townsend Plan clubs of elderly voters. President Franklin D. Roosevelt's Committee on Economic Security could not afford to ignore the strong and growing agitation for old age benefits which the Townsend plan had stirred up. Its own recommendation for a national old age retirement program would have to be acceptable to a public fired up by Townsend if it were to succeed as legislation. According to Schlesinger, "the mounting Townsendite clamor in late 1934 and early 1935 certainly improved the opportunity for inserting sweeping old-age insurance recommendations in the social security bill."[13] The enactment of the old age retirement program as part of the broad 1935 Social Security Act constituted in essence a rejection of the Townsend plan in favor of the now-existing program. Realistic policy alternatives which were presented by opposing factions after 1935, despite the existence of the laissez-faire and expansionist philosophies noted by Myers, were much less global in scope and posed much less of a threat to the continued development of a more comprehensive and liberal retirement benefit program.

Findings

Title II of the Social Security Act of 1935 is the basis for the Social Security program of cash benefits in old age and retirement. In the years following its enactment, there was a constant flow of legislation to change the program, primarily in the direction of expansion and liberalization. Coverage was extended to occupational groups well beyond the wage and salary workers included under the original legislation. The benefit computation formula was

---

[13] Schlesinger, The Coming of the New Deal, p. 307.

liberalized and other changes made to produce larger benefits; in addition, various kinds of dependents' benefits were added to those of the worker. The earnings test governing the amount of benefit lost in cases where the worker may be retired, but has some earned income in a given month or months, was eased. Authorization for the use of general tax revenues, if necessary, was enacted, although later repealed. The program continued to be financed by wage and payroll taxes; hand in hand with the enactment of more and larger benefits, there were legislated increases in both the contribution rate and the earnings base. These changes provided more program revenue per worker, while the expanded coverage meant more workers and employers were paying taxes into the Social Security trust fund for old age and retirement benefits.

Program executives guided policymaking for the Social Security program according to the goals which they envisioned for it, both minding and molding public opinion as they went. Very few outsiders understood the technical details of the program, so that the expertise of the executives was appreciated and respected. Program executives worked consistently toward an expanded and more liberal old age benefit program, understanding nevertheless that change would happen piecemeal and incrementally. They sought and obtained the support of key Congressional, business, labor and public leaders. They were attentive to public reaction to the program, but it is likely that they shaped that reaction to a great extent by skillful presentation of the program and their proposals for change.

The small group of key Social Security program executives were, in Dahl's formulation of the policymaking hierarchy, extremely powerful subleaders. As discussed in Chapter I of this study, the influence of the most powerful subleaders and that of the leaders themselves (Lindblom's "proximate policy makers") merge imperceptibly together. The Social Security program executives and their Congressional backers formed a close unity, with outside business, labor and public leaders as the next larger, inner circle of program allies.

One of the public leaders who was active in the inner circles of Social Security policymaking throughout its first quarter century was Dr. Eveline M. Burns. In the next chapter, the study examines her work and her efforts to provide professional leadership with respect to the Social Security old age retirement program.

CHAPTER V

ATTEMPTING TO INFLUENCE SOCIAL POLICY: DR. BURNS' ACTIVITIES WITH RESPECT TO OLD AGE RETIREMENT INCOME POLICIES AND THE SOCIAL SECURITY ACT

In the last chapter, the study examined the legislative changes which were enacted in the old age and retirement benefit program in Social Security for the twenty-five year period after its inception in 1935. It found that there had been considerable expansion and liberalization in its coverage and provisions, which was due in large part to expert program executives who worked closely with policy makers and public opinion to help guide and shape the program. This chapter will examine how Dr. Burns attempted to influence the nature of that change through professional leadership. It looks at her activities in three dimensions: as a writer, as a direct advocate, and in an organizational setting.

The Scholarly Route: Researcher and Writer

Dr. Burns started writing about the Social Security Act literally from its inception. She did not do this haphazardly, but from the strong belief that informed public opinion was a powerful force and that she had a role to play in providing information to the public. As she wrote in 1936, one year after the passage of the Social Security legislation,

> in a democratic society voters are most likely to choose intelligently when they are fully informed as to the implications of the available alternatives. . . . It is the function of the economist to use his technique to explain to those who have no time to specialize in these problems the probable economic consequences of proposed measures.[1]

---

[1] Burns, Toward Social Security, pp. vi-vii.

The statement comes from a book written by Dr. Burns to explain to a lay audience the provisions of the new legislation and to place them in a policy context. In that book, Toward Social Security, she painstakingly explains what types of income security will be provided as a result of the Social Security Act, how they will be paid for, and who will be eligible to receive the benefits. Beyond the facts, however, she also makes clear in what areas she believes that the Act comes up short and could be improved at a future date. With respect to old age retirement, she deals in the book with the inadequacy of coverage, the unfairness of the earnings test, the low level of benefits, and the failure to include the use of general revenues. These four areas of concern continue as themes in her writings on old age retirement throughout the following decades. Woven through those writings, also, is the theme of the need for informed public opinion and public participation in decision making on Social Security policies and programs. Her writings, therefore, must be considered as an attempt to influence public opinion and, thereby, to influence the direction of public policy in addition to their manifest purpose of providing factual information and elucidating issues for an interested lay audience.

The issues which Dr. Burns pinpointed in 1936--coverage, the earnings test, benefit levels, and the use of general revenues--persisted over time because of their importance as determinants of social and economic policies and values in the United States. She realized that a nation's policies and programs must take diverse needs into balanced consideration, but that the mark of a humane society is the attention it pays to the needs of the poorest and least powerful. Thus, coverage expansions and higher benefit levels were important as indicators of basic social values as well as being an economically sound way of helping to insure that people would have adequate income to live on after retirement and would be less likely to become public charges at that time. The earnings test, while important at its inception as a way to open up jobs for younger workers in a tight labor market, became of questionable use as the economy improved, as the number of aged in the population grew larger, and as the needs of the aged for income and for continued social productivity became more evident. The use of general revenues would have provided a base for a broader, national social insurance program which, in all likelihood, would eventually have covered more people and provided better and more diverse benefits than a program financed exclusively through wage and payroll taxes. The use of general revenues if and when wage and payroll taxes were insufficient would also have provided an assured revenue base to finance benefits. However, the question of requiring the population at large to assume part of the financing burden for Social Security met with both political and philosophical opposition over the years.

The limitations on Social Security coverage which were contained in the 1935 legislation were perceived by Dr. Burns as inequitable and leading to an inadequate old age retirement program. She was also aware, however, that not all of the omissions were unreasonable at that time because of technical shortcomings, that some were a matter of political feasibility in order to get the Act passed, and that the Act, once passed, was not graven in stone. By 1936, Dr. Burns was urging in Toward Social Security that changes be made in Social Security coverage. "To provide anything like complete security in old age the Act must be changed in the near future to take in as many as possible of the employments now excluded."[2] She was particularly concerned that

> while the Act provides secure annuities for highly paid people who might be expected to be perfectly able to provide for their own old age, it fails to provide them for a great many people whose need is only too obvious.[3]

The two major occupational groups excluded from Social Security coverage in 1935 were agricultural

---

[2] Ibid., pp. 27-28.

[3] Ibid., pp. 24-25.

and domestic workers. Also excluded were employees of government and nonprofit organizations, self-employed individuals, people such as housewives who did not receive wages for their services, and others not gainfully or regularly employed. The practical reason for the exclusion of agricultural and domestic workers from coverage was the administrative difficulty of tracking the earnings of workers in these two groups on a regular and continuing basis; the workers in both of these groups are widely scattered, change employers frequently, and have a large number of employers relative to the number of workers. Dr. Burns acknowledged that administrative problems related to the question of coverage for agricultural and domestic workers existed, but also believed that "these differences may be overcome in the future and some of them are probably exaggerated."[4] She told her readers that "many other countries have found it possible to include both agriculture and domestic service in contributory old-age annuities systems."[5] It did not escape Dr. Burns that the exclusion of these employment sectors, however valid the administrative reasons for doing so, weighed particularly heavily upon women and blacks, two demographic groups largely employed in agricultural and domestic work. She went so far as to say that "this part of the Security Act has been described as a plan to provide security for white male wage earners, and there is some truth in the charge."[6] As for the exclusion of employees of nonprofit organizations, Dr. Burns saw that provision as a bow to political expediency at the time of the Act's passage.

> There is no reason, apart from political pressure exercised by representatives of the employers concerned, why workers in the employment of religious, charitable, scientific,

---

[4] Ibid., pp. 143-144.

[5] Ibid.

[6] Ibid., p. 27.

> literary, and educational organizations should be denied unemployment compensation or old-age annuities.[7]

She strongly urged that public policy be changed so that all three of these groups--agricultural and domestic workers and employees of nonprofit organizations--could be make eligible for coverage under Social Security old age retirement and other programs.

> The Act itself must be amended at the earliest possible opportunity. . . . Workers in non-profit-making concerns should at once be placed on an equality with their fellows working for profit-making employers, and brought within the scope of the old-age annuities and unemployment compensation plans. As soon as the Social Security Board has laid the foundations of its adminstrative procedures, the remaining employees excluded from the old-age annuities and unemployment compensation plans should be included.[8]

Several years after the publication of Toward Social Security, Dr. Burns authored another major document in which she dealt with the issue of Social Security coverage. She was the Director of Research for the Committee on Long-Range Work and Relief Policies, a committee appointed by President Franklin D. Roosevelt's National Resources Planning Board to review a decade of experience and to present recommendations on meeting the needs of the nation's disadvantaged citizens. The committee report, Security, Work, and Relief Policies, was written by Dr. Burns and was published in 1942. The expansions of coverage which she had advocated in Toward Social Security in 1936 had not yet been enacted and she again focused attention on workers in the agricultural, domestic and nonprofit sectors. With respect to the first two of these categories,

---

[7] Ibid., p. 145.

[8] Ibid., pp. 237-238.

however, she was no longer content merely to press for their inclusion as covered groups in the Social Security old age retirement program. Her change of emphasis was related to the realization that other Social Security provisions and other public policies, if unchanged, could make inclusion under Social Security unproductive or even counterproductive for workers in those fields.

The shift in focus from pressing for the inclusion of agricultural and domestic workers as soon as administratively feasible to a position that such coverage must be linked to other policy changes showed Dr. Burns' foremost concern for people and for the potential effects of social and public policies on their wellbeing. She had come to realize that

> extension of coverage to occupations at present excluded from the scope of the program has frequently been held to be the best method by which the major difficulties of those not yet insured could be overcome. But many of the occupations still to be covered are those in which wages are low and employment frequently intermittent, such as agricultural labor and domestic service.[9]

Those employment conditions meant that Social Security coverage might be of little or no benefit to many agricultural or domestic workers, in terms of the retirement income which they could hope to receive, even if they were permitted to participate in the program. Dr. Burns emphasized this point in the 1942 Report.

> Technical and economic considerations admittedly impose obstacles to the extension of the social-insurance type of security. The exclusion of agricultural and domestic workers has been due, in part at least, to the difficulties of devising administrative

---

[9] Burns, Security, Work, and Relief Policies, p. 211.

> mechanisms for the collection of contributions and payment of benefits and the necessary controls for assuring compliance with the eligibility requirements. But a more serious obstacle to the general provision of economic security through the social-insurance method is presented by the low level of earnings and irregularity of employment of many sections of the working population. So long as eligibility for benefits and the amount of benefit payable are directly related to a worker's past earnings and employment record, the formal coverage of low-paid and irregularly employed workers in a social-insurance program may be a dubious advantage. For although legally covered they may not qualify for benefits, or if eligible they may receive lower payments than they could secure under some other program. So long as present benefit and eligibility formulas are retained, therefore, the fact that the system does not embrace all of the working population is not necessarity a weakness of the social-insurance system.[10]

Since employees of nonprofit organizations were not, as a group, subject to the extremely low wages and intermittent conditions of employment which characterized the agricultural and domestic sectors, Dr. Burns continued to press without reservation for their inclusion under Social Security. With respect to these three major groups excluded from coverage, therefore, the 1942 Report made the following recommendation:

> Coverage should be extended to employees of nonprofit corporations. Additional groups of employees should be covered as rapidly as it can be demonstrated that they will receive adequate or significant benefits from the system.[11]

The thrust of the policy recommendation continued to

---

[10] Ibid., p. 459. (Italics in original text.)

[11] Ibid., pp. 547-548.

be to strengthen Social Security and to make it more widely available. The slight shift in focus from 1936 was to urge that policy changes be packaged where necessary to achieve the desired results, rather than be taken in isolation if the latter course was not likely to produce the hoped-for effect. The goal was still to achieve coverage for agricultural and domestic workers, with the added dimension of concern that income security through Social Security coverage, for these as for other groups of workers, exist in fact as well as in name.

After the completion of her work with the National Resources Planning Board, Dr. Burns continued to think and write about the need for passing legislation to extend Social Security coverage to the large numbers of workers not covered by the 1935 Act, for whom nothing had been done since in that regard. In 1949, The American Social Security System was published. In that book, Dr. Burns presented at length the arguments for expansion of coverage to various groups of workers and the changes which had occurred since 1935 to make such expansion more feasible, desirable, or practical by the end of the 1940s. She argued that fourteen years had brought about many changes in public attitudes and program capabilities, that many of the original reasons for limiting coverage were no longer valid, and that, on the contrary, there was an increasing awareness of the disadvantages of retaining the limitations on coverage imposed in 1935. As in her previous writings, Dr. Burns paid considerable attention to the lack of coverage for agricultural and domestic workers and employees of nonprofit organizations. Looking beyond those groups, however, she noted that the 1935 Act also did not cover federal, state or local government employees, the self-employed, or members of the armed forces. All of the foregoing exclusions amounted to a considerable number of jobs. "It has been estimated that only 3 out of every 5 jobs," she wrote,

> are covered by OASI [Old Age and Survivors Insurance]. The most obvious impact of the coverage and minimum earnings requirement,

> therefore, is on those workers whose sole or primary source of income is from uncovered employment. These groups are denied all OASI benefits.[12]

She went on to make the point that the effect of having so many jobs not covered by Social Security is compounded by the fact that job changes by individuals in the course of a lifetime mean that many more workers are affected by the limitations than would appear at first blush. "A second major disadvantage of the incomplete coverage of OASI lies in its effect upon workers who move between covered and uncovered employment."[13] In addition to the obvious economic effect on individuals who move between these two types of employment, Dr. Burns pointed out that the distinction between covered and uncovered employment "has the further disadvantage of impeding free labor mobility."[14] Having thus made the case for expanded coverage from the perspective of individual workers who would not be eligible for benefits or whose benefits might be reduced as a consequence of the existing law, Dr. Burns appealed with a final argument to the self-interest of agricultural states. The continued exclusion of the large numbers of agricultural workers from those states, which were often among the poorer states of the nation, would in the long run mean higher state costs for Old Age Assistance programs for the elderly poor, since so many of their workers would not have Social Security benefits upon retirement and would have to fall back on state-financed public assistance programs instead.[15]

After presenting all of the disadvantages of continuing to exclude major types of employment from

---

[12] Burns, The American Social Security System, p. 71.

[13] Ibid., p. 72.

[14] Ibid., p. 75.

[15] Ibid.

coverage under Social Security, Dr. Burns marshalled arguments to show why the limitations were no longer necessary. She pointed out that the administrative difficulties envisioned in 1935 in connection with coverage of agricultural and domestic workers and the self-employed had waned considerably in importance, given that government agencies, employers, and workers now had eleven years of experience and familiarity with the operation of the program.[16] Nonprofit organizations no longer feared that paying the employer's portion of Social Security taxes might serve as a precedent and make them liable for other forms of taxation.[17] There had been study since 1935 of ways by which civil service retirement benefits for federal government employees could be coordinated with Social Security.[18] Finally, since the federal government cannot levy a tax on states and localities, it had been suggested that state and local government employees could constitutionally be covered through the use of a voluntary compact.[19]

Dr. Burns summoned up, in the 1949 book, all of the arguments for expansion of Social Security coverage. She noted, but did not highlight as she had done in the 1942 Report, the need to link such coverage to improved benefits for low-paid workers. She wrote, without much elaboration, that "extended coverage, to be a net gain to some of the workers concerned, therefore involves a liberalization of the benefit formula."[20] The heavy emphasis in 1949, however, was on the need for expanding coverage, its feasibility, and the increasing support for that action on the part of knowledgeable people both inside and outside of government.

---

[16] Ibid., p. 78.

[17] Ibid., pp. 81-82.

[18] Ibid., p. 83.

[19] Ibid., p. 84.

[20] Ibid., p. 85.

It is evident from the foregoing discussion of the limited coverage of OASI that many of the original reasons for excluding certain types of employment are no longer operative. The obstacles which involved administrative problems appear to have been largely solved. Interest in the program and demand for coverage on the part of those now excluded have greatly increased, and in a number of cases employer opposition is significantly less vociferous. At the same time there is a growing awareness of the disadvantages of limited coverage. One of these is the social inequity of denying the right to this preferred form of security to groups whose need is great and who meanwhile (to the extent that payroll taxes are reflected in higher prices) contribute indirectly toward the benefits of those now covered. Another disadvantage lies in the risks to eligibility and reduction of benefits resulting from movement between covered and uncovered work; a third is the difference between the states in the extent to which OASI contributes toward a solution to the problem of old-age dependency. Furthermore, it has been pointed out that more nearly universal coverage would remove one obstacle to the introduction of a subsidy from general tax revenues, namely, the inequity of making public funds available to only a limited group of wage earners.

It is therefore not surprising that all groups which have studied the program have regarded limited coverage as the outstanding weakness of the OASI program.[21]

The improvements in benefit coverage which Dr. Burns had been advocating in her writings were enacted in large part in 1950. Social Security legislation passed in that year, as noted in Chapter IV above, extended coverage to major new groups of workers. These included regularly employed agricultural and domestic workers, employees of nonprofit organizations, state and local government

---

[21] Ibid., pp. 85-86.

employees not covered under their own government retirement system, and nonfarm self-employed individuals other than members of professional groups. Additional legislation in 1954 and 1956 brought coverage to self-employed agricultural workers and professionals other than physicians, to members of the armed forces, and to additional state and local government employees, among others.

While the inadequacy of coverage was a major theme in Dr. Burns' writings from the passage of the Social Security Act until the passage of additional legislation bringing most of the excluded groups into the program, it was not the only theme. As mentioned earlier in this chapter, three other issues which concerned her over the years and which appeared regularly in her writings on Social Security old age retirement were the unfairness of the earnings test, the low level of benefits generally, and the failure of the legislation to provide for the use of general revenues to pay part of the costs.

The earnings test, as enacted in the 1935 legislation, required that the Social Security monthly benefit be reduced in its entirety for any month in which a retiree had earned income, regardless of the amount of income or age of the beneficiary. Dr. Burns deplored this aspect of the Social Security retirement program and wrote as early as 1936 in favor of changing it, in Toward Social Security.

> Why should a worker who has regularly paid contributions not be permitted to run his private life as he wishes after the age of sixty-five? The object of imposing this condition was to compel older people to give up their jobs in favor of the young. But it is questionable whether it is fair to use the contributory annuities system for this purpose, especially since the annuities to be paid to older people in the years immediately ahead will

be very small.[22]

A minor liberalization of the earnings test was enacted in 1939, allowing retirees to have up to $14.99 monthly in wages, which they could earn and keep without its affecting their retirement benefit.

Dr. Burns continued to write in favor of changing or eliminating the earnings test. She reiterated in 1949 her belief that the low level of Social Security benefits did not make them a feasible alternative to earnings and that, therefore, the earnings test would not encourage older workers to retire, which was the primary purpose of including it in 1935. Further, by 1949 she did not even regard the encouragement of retirement as a desirable purpose. She believed that the economic production of the aged would be of increasing importance to the country as well as being beneficial for the aged individuals themselves, from both the psychological and the financial perspectives.

> Decisions as to the specific nature and the desirability in principle of a retirement clause would seem to depend upon the answers to two major questions: how far can the community afford to dispense with the contribution to production that might be made by a group whose numbers and relative importance are increasing steadily, and to what extent is it desirable, in the interests of the individuals concerned or for the maintenance of certain social values, to encourage the aged to continue working as long as possible?[23]

In answering her own questions, Dr. Burns made the case for either eliminating the earnings test or drastically changing its form and application. She backed up her case by noting that she was not alone in calling for such change.

---

[22] Burns, <u>Toward Social Security</u>, pp. 19-20.

[23] Burns, <u>The American Social Security System</u>, pp. 87-88.

> On the first issue, the future growth in the proportion which persons over 65 will form of the total population . . . . would seem to suggest that it would be to the interest of those under 65 to encourage the aged to continue contributing to production as long as possible, or at least not to discourage them from doing so. On the second issue there seems to be considerable evidence that the welfare of the aged themselves is undermined by enforced idleness. Furthermore, if it is desired to sustain the spirit of independence and initiative, the form of the retirement provision which now denies all benefit when earnings exceed a certain amount should be replaced by a sliding scale, which reduced benefits in proportion to earnings so that up to a certain income level a beneficiary would always be better off by earning than by living on benefit alone. For these reasons, proposals have been made either that there should be no retirement clause or that it should be limited to those under the age of 70, that the sliding scale should be adopted, and that the amount of earnings which would involve no benefit deduction should be substantially increased.[24]

In 1950, the year after the above paragraph was written, legislation was enacted to exempt beneficiaries aged seventy-five or older from the earnings test; in 1954, the age for exemption was further lowered to seventy-two. In addition, the amount of monthly earnings permitted without reduction in benefits was raised to $50 in 1950, $75 in 1952, and $80 in 1954.

The issue of the earnings test did not disappear with the liberalizations of the early 1950s. Questions continued to be raised about the desirability of having a retirement test versus simply providing benefits automatically upon the attainment of a specified age, such as sixty-five

---

[24] Ibid.

years old. In 1956, in Social Security and Public Policy, Dr. Burns wrote that, by that time,

> some of the most acute differences of opinion turned around the question of whether an old-age security system should pay benefits automatically on attainment of some specific age or should be conditioned on age plus retirement from the labor market.[25]

She did not take one side or the other on that issue, but instead laid out the conditions for the optimal implementation of either alternative, should public policy lead in that direction. If it were decided that benefits should be provided automatically, as a right, then Dr. Burns' concern, from both an economic and a social standpoint, was with the choice of an age for the receipt of benefits. Rather than advocating a specific age, she suggested that the general capacity to find or retain employment among members of a given age group should be a determining factor.[26] If, on the other hadd, Social Security benefits were to continue to be conditioned on age plus retirement from the labor market and, therefore, a retirement test were to be retained, then she urged that a sliding scale for benefit reduction replace the all-or-nothing policy which had been enacted in 1935.

> But a provision like that operating in the United States, whereby any earnings in excess of the statutory maximum amount result in the denial of the entire benefit for the month in question, will discourage employment unless it yields substantially more than the benefit plus the permitted amount of earnings. Efforts to avoid this difficulty by, as in the United States, continually raising the amount of exempt earnings, would, if carried far, destroy the effectiveness of the retirement clause for

---

[25] Eveline M. Burns, Social Security and Public Policy (New York: McGraw-Hill, 1956), p. 97.

[26] Ibid., pp. 101-102.

> substantial numbers of beneficiaries. The alternative solution would be to abandon the "all or nothing" type of retirement test and substitute for it a sliding scale whereby specified amounts of earnings would lead to a somewhat smaller reduction of the benefit. In this way, within the limits of some defined total monthly income the beneficiary would always be better off by some degree of employment.[27]

The sliding scale proposal was, in fact, the course taken by policymakers within a few years of Dr. Burns' above discussion of it. In 1958, legislation raised the permitted amount of monthly earnings to $100. Then, in 1960, subsequent legislation introduced the sliding scale concept by stipulating that, for the next $300 earned in a year, benefits would be reduced by $1 for each $2 of those earnings, instead of being taken away entirely for the month or months.

The issues of both coverage and the earnings test, as Dr. Burns pointed out in her writings, were affected by low benefit levels. Low benefits made coverage useless or nearly so to low-paid workers and were counterproductive in terms of the earnings test goal of encouraging retirement. A more fundamental indictment of low benefit levels which appeared in her writings and grew stronger over the years was that they represented a failure of public policy to meet the desirable and desired goal of providing economic security through social insurance to the bulk of aged retirees. As early as 1936, Dr. Burns wrote of her dissatisfaction with the benefit levels provided for in the 1935 Act, although she took great care not to be so critical as to sour her readers on the Act itself. Noting that she was "critical of the Social Security Act in regard both to the amount of individual security provided and to the methods of provision," she nevertheless expressed her strong conviction "that reforms are not unworthy of support

---

[27] Ibid., p. 109.

merely because they are incomplete."[28] It was clear in 1936 that Dr. Burns wanted to generate public support and approval for the new Social Security Act, particularly in light of the earlier popularity of the Townsend movement, but that she was also disappointed by the low levels of retirement benefits provided by the Act and anticipated that other people would have a similar reaction. She sincerely lauded the new legislation: "The federal annuities and the federal-state old-age pensions together go far to remove from aging people the specter of dependency."[29] Nevertheless, she understood and sympathized that

> the relatively low level of the benefits provided will cause disappointment in many quarters. The $40 to $50 a month likely to be received by the average retired worker under the federal annuities plan, or the monthly pension of $30 under the state old-age pension laws, will seem to many to be very poor substitutes for the $200 a month which the Townsend plan promises to all aged people.[30]

In the 1942 Report, as discussed above, Dr. Burns emphasized that low benefit levels not only did not afford enough protection, but also made pursuit of other Social Security goals a more questionable activity.

> So long as eligibility for benefits and the amount of benefit payable are directly related to a worker's past earnings and employment record, the formal coverage of low-paid and irregularly employed workers in a social-insurance program may be a dubious advantage.[31]

---

[28] Burns, Toward Social Security, p. vii.

[29] Ibid., p. 122.

[30] Ibid.

[31] Burns, Security, Work, and Relief Policies, p. 459.

Given that benefits were quite low for even the average worker, they could be expected to provide little or nothing for the low-paid worker. The Report recommended that "continuing study should be given to the feasibility of revising the benefit formulas."[32]

By the late 1940s, with the war years behind and general prosperity on the rise in the country, public clamor had also risen for improved Social Security benefits. In her writings, Dr. Burns reaffirmed her own, longstanding point of view on the need for better benefits.

> Since the purpose of the Old-Age and Survivors Insurance system is to assure a minimum of security and independence to the recipients, it is important to assess the adequacy of the payments yielded by the benefit formula.[33]

She bolstered her position by pointing out the many voices, both inside and outside of government, which were by now advocating the same thing.

> The low level and relative insignificance of the contribution to family security of OASI benefit have given rise to many proposals for liberalization which have become more insistent with the rising cost of living. Labor organizations, federal agencies such as the National Resources Planning Board and the Social Security Administration, organizations of state and local public welfare administrators such as the American Public Welfare Association, and citizens' organizations such as the National Planning Association, have all urged amendment of the act to provide for increased monthly payments.
>
> The most specific of the proposals have

---

32 Ibid., p. 548.

33 Burns, The American Social Security System, p. 96.

> been those embodied in the Wagner-Murray-Dingell Bill originally introduced into Congress in 1943, and those made by the Social Security Administration and the Advisory Council on Social Security in 1948.[34]

In 1950, Congress finally acted positively on the concerns of Dr. Burns and others about the low level of Social Security benefits in general and the particular plight of low-paid workers with respect to the benefits available to them. In that year, legislation was passed to increase benefits by about 77 percent, ranging from a 100 percent increase at the lowest benefit level to a 50 percent increase at the highest level. Benefit increases continued to be enacted throughout the 1950s, by approximately 12 1/2 percent in 1952, 13 percent in 1954 and, finally, another 7 percent in 1958. By that time, given that legislation had satisfactorily resolved for the present the problem of low benefit levels, Dr. Burns' attention had shifted from benefit levels per se to the question of how to maintain benefit adequacy over time in the face of general price or wage changes. She explained to her readers in 1956 that

> about the only available remedy is to provide for an across-the-board increase in benefits, either on a planned or an emergency basis. This happened in the United States in 1950 and again in 1952 and 1954, when blanket increases were made in both current and future OASI benefits.[35]

One solution, she suggested, would be the enactment of legislation providing for automatic cost-of-living increases. A public policy decision to provide automatic benefit increases, however, would require a concomitant decision about financing. She pointed out that

---

[34] Ibid., pp. 102-103.

[35] Burns, Social Security and Public Policy, p. 50.

> where automatic cost-of-living increases are applied to benefits already awarded, no corresponding increase in revenue will be secured. Whatever cost is involved must be carried by current contributors to the fund or, as it is in some countries which have adopted this device, by the general taxpayer.[36]

Dr. Burns had, in fact, long been an advocate for the use of general tax revenues to cover part of the costs of the Social Security old age retirement benefit program.

The question of the use of general revenues in the Social Security program was an issue on which Dr. Burns disagreed strongly with President Roosevelt. He wanted a self-sustaining program; she believed that reliance solely on wage and payroll taxes meant that the costs of the program would fall disproportionately upon the poor. After the passage of the Act, which followed the President's call for a self-sustaining program, Dr. Burns felt free to express her disagreement.

> If we agree with President Roosevelt that the self-sustaining social insurance method is the only sound way of financing annuities and unemployment compensation benefits, we are therefore saying that we believe that the poor should be compelled to pay most of the cost of helping the poor.[37]

She did not disagree with the use of wage and payroll taxes in general; rather, she believed in the contributory principle which they represented and felt that their use would lead to a stronger program over time. Her objection was to a total reliance upon those taxes to meet program costs. As she wrote in 1936,

---

[36] Ibid., p. 55.

[37] Burns, <u>Toward Social Security</u>, p. 161.

> beyond a certain point taxes on employers have undesirable economic consequences and taxes on workers become an intolerable burden on an already low standard of living. This point may be reached before enough money has been obtained to provide adequate security. The solution is not to stop short of full security but to provide the additional funds necessary out of general taxation.[38]

She again pressed the issue in the report which she authored for presentation to President Roosevelt's National Resources Planning Board. The recommendations for strengthening the old-age and survivors insurance system contained in that 1942 Report included the following: "The general principle of a governmental contribution to the costs of the program should be specifically embodied in legislation."[39]

The general use of general tax revenues to make up any financial deficit in Social Security, but not to pay regular program costs, was authorized by Congress in 1944. That authorization was subsequently repealed in new legislation passed by Congress in 1950. The issue of using general revenues to pay program costs, however, did not go away, either then or later. In 1949, remarking on the wage and payroll tax financing of Social Security benefits, Dr. Burns wrote: "Whether these taxes will continue to be the sole source of revenue in later years appears to be as yet undecided."[40] She believed that the extension of coverage, bringing additional groups of workers into the Social Security program, might help to move policy in the direction of use of general revenues, since that action would substantially eliminate arguments about "the inequity

---

[38] Ibid., pp. 174-175.

[39] Burns, Security, Work, and Relief Policies, p. 548.

[40] Burns, The American Social Security System, p. 65.

of making public funds available to only a limited group of wage earners."[41] Although, as this study has pointed out, legislation throughout the 1950s brought most of the excluded groups of workers into the Social Security program and achieved something very close to universal coverage, those changes in coverage nevertheless did not lead to changes in the legislative policy on the use of general revenues. By 1956, Dr. Burns seemed resigned to the idea that it was not likely that general tax revenues would be used in the Social Security program in the near future, but, as always, she took the optimistic and long-range view of the possibility of eventual change.

> Even more important is the fact that the range of risks covered by social insurance systems is still relatively narrow in the United States as compared to many other countries of an equally advanced stage of economic development. Were more risks to be covered, and this type of protection extended to all or almost all the population, it seems likely that in America too there would be an irresistible demand for a contribution from the general revenues to the social insurance programs.[42]

The failure of the United States to cover more risks in its social insurance programs, to extend those protections to more people, and to use general revenues to cover the costs may have been a disappointment to Dr. Burns, but it could not have been entirely surprising. As will be discussed later in this chapter, her 1942 National Resources Planning Board Report calling for a comprehensive, national system of economic security was decried as paternalistic, destructive of states' rights, too expensive and reflective of undesirable foreign ideologies. Neither American business interests nor

---

[41] Ibid., p. 86.

[42] Burns, Social Security and Public Policy, p. 176.

the public at large have been ready to accept a social welfare system which imposes heavy taxes and covers most of life's economic risks. The use of general revenues to pay regular Social Security program costs has been perceived as a foot in the door to that unwanted, broader program and has therefore met with resistance over the years.

In summary, the policy positions advocated by Eveline M. Burns in her writings on Social Security old age retirement benefits between the years of 1935 and 1960 met with considerable, although not total, legislative success. This section has examined four of the issues on which she wrote: extension of coverage, the earnings test, low benefit levels and the use of general tax revenues in the Social Security program. It has shown that the changes which she urged were, in large part, adopted. Coverage was extended to include almost all major groups of workers, with the exception of federal employees covered by their own retirement system. The earnings test was not eliminated, but legislation was enacted to exempt beneficiaries above a specified age from the test. In the case of those for whom the earnings test continued to apply, some earnings were permitted without any reduction in benefits and a sliding scale of benefit reduction was introduced for earnings above the permissible exempt amount. Benefit levels were also the subject of legislative change. In the 1950s, the levels were improved considerably across the board. In addition, the single largest increase was constructed so that benefits at the low end of the scale received a much higher percentage increase than benefits at the higher end. Only with respect to the use of general tax revenues was there no significant change. In the three other areas studied, the policy changes envisioned as desirable by Dr. Burns early on and advocated by her in her writings through the years became, in time, the object of considerable public support and were eventually written into law.

Dr. Burns was not, of course, the only person advocating Social Security changes over the years, nor was she doing it only by means of her writings. In the next section, the study examines some of the direct, one-on-one personal associations and relationships which helped Dr. Burns to gain attention for the changes which she hoped to see enacted in the Social Security program.

The Direct Advocacy Route: Personal Friend and Acquaintance

It was shown in Chapter IV that many of the changes which were made over the years in the Social Security program were guided by an inner circle of policy makers and their close allies. The core of that group consisted of program executives and Congressmen; business, labor and lay leaders were also part of the larger group and played a role in terms of both policy discussions and public support. Eveline M. Burns became one of the group of friends and acquaintances involved in Social Security decision making through a combination of luck, skill and personal attributes.

Eveline M. Burns and her husband Arthur, both economists, had come to the United States in 1926 and spent much of the first few years in such economically oriented, intellectual circles as the Brookings School in Washington, D.C. There, and also in New York, Dr. Burns first started to meet and become known to people who were thinking and working in the fields of social and economic policy in this country. By the time a realization of the need for social insurance had taken hold and steps were being taken to make it a reality in the early 1930s, she had already met some of the people who were to play a part in that activity and must have impressed them with her ability. By 1934, by which time she was a faculty member at Columbia University, she was invited to join the staff of the Committee on Economic Security as a subordinate to Meredith Givens. He was in charge of the group looking at work programs for the Committee and was someone with whom she had collaborated earlier on consultant work in New York.[43] Her role as a staff member of the Committee on Economic Security brought her into direct contact with the people involved in developing all of the proposed pieces of the Social Security Act, even though her own actual assignment was limited to work programs.

In addition to the various contacts she had made and was making in Washington, she had become well acquainted in New York with Abraham Epstein, founder of the organization first known as the American Association for Old Age Security and later as the American Association for Social Security. Epstein, an outspoken advocate for economic security for the aged in the years before and after the passage of the Social Security Act, had been in one of her Columbia University seminars. He subsequently arranged for her participation in both the ongoing affairs and the annual conferences of his organization.[44] Dr. Burns was asked by Epstein in 1933 to serve on the National Advisory Committee of his American Association for Old Age Security, which gave her a voice in the development of the policy agenda for that advocacy organization. In 1936, she was elected to be a Vice-President of the by-then-renamed American Association for Social Security.

After the passage of the Social Security Act, a government board was appointed to take charge of implementing the new legislation and setting the mechanisms in place for the new programs. Dr. Burns was hired as a consultant to help with that task and to set up and run their training programs. That job brought her into frequent contact with John Winant, the former Governor of New Hampshire who was the first Chairman of the new Social Security Board. Although there was no policymaking power attached to her job, she found that he often asked her questions and listened willingly to her answers and ideas. The

---

[43] Interviews with Dr. Burns, 12 June 1982 and 16 January 1984, and personal papers from her files.

[44] Interviews with Dr. Burns, 12 June 1982 and 27 May 1984.

relationship with Winant was typical of Dr. Burns' relationships over the years with people who had the policymaking power which she herself did not have; that is, she was smart, she was affable, and she had his ear. As she phrased it, he was "an intellectual chap" who liked to think about all the questions. "I was a consultant and running their training program and dealt with him a lot. He was always asking me questions."[45]

Arthur Altmeyer, who was a member of the original Social Security Board under Winant, took over as its Chairman in 1937. Although he was a far more opinionated person than Winant, she had taken care not to offend him in prior years and was therefore kept on as a participant in the early years of Social Security program implementation.[46] Taking care not to offend did not necessarily mean keeping quiet about what she believed. With Altmeyer, as with Winant earlier, Dr. Burns continued to express her ideas on Social Security Act program issues. Altmeyer and she frequently argued "on one thing or another," but here, again, her ability to get on with people on a personal basis afforded her continuing access to the halls of power and the ears of the powerful.[47]

Dr. Burns' attachment to Social Security's inner circle was also enhanced by the appointment of Molly Dewson to the Social Security Board in 1937.[48] In the early 1920s, while still writing her dissertation at the London School of Economics, Dr. Burns had written to Molly Dewson for some materials that the latter had prepared on the question of a minimum wage. The two women began a correspondence and, after Dr. Burns came to the United States to live,

---

[45] Interview with Dr. Burns, 16 January 1984.

[46] Ibid.

[47] Ibid.

[48] Derthick, p. 34.

they became close friends. Ida Merriam, who had met Dr. Burns in Washington, D.C. in the 1920s, was another of the circle of friends actively involved in Social Security policy issues from the program's early years.[49]

Three additional important associations, in terms of Social Security policymaking, were Dr. Burns' relationships with Robert Myers, Robert Ball and Wilbur Cohen. Robert Myers was a key figure in Social Security policymaking whose expertise was in determining and laying out proposal costs and alternatives. It was he who prepared the actuarial estimates for the 1935 Act and he was the program's chief actuary from 1947 to 1970.[50] Dr. Burns developed a solid professional relationship with him during the years following the passage of the Social Security Act, when she was a frequent consultant in Washington to the Social Security Board and he was then the assistant to the chief actuary.[51] Although Dr. Burns and Myers were not personally close, and in spite of the fact that they held different beliefs as to what the Social Security program should be, they maintained a working relationship throughout the years in which he frequently reviewed her writings. He did this, Myers notes, "sometimes at her request and other times on my own volition."[52] Myers may not have shared Dr. Burns' views on Social Security, but it should not go unremarked that he willingly

---

[49] Interviews with Dr. Burns, 12 June 1982 and 16 January 1984, during which the author also learned that Molly Dewson had been President of the Consumers' League of New York when Frances Perkins, who later became President Roosevelt's Secretary of Labor, was its Executive Director. Ida Merriam held various posts in the Social Security Administration, including direction of its research program.

[50] Derthick, p. 55.

[51] Interview with Dr. Burns, 27 May 1984.

[52] Robert J. Myers, personal letter to the author.

read her books and papers and helped her make sure that she was presenting correct facts to support her policy positions for more than forty years.

Robert Ball and Wilbur Cohen were more than just professional relationships in Dr. Burns' life; they became her personal friends as well.[53] These two men, together with Arthur Altmeyer, "were variously civil servants, political appointees, and private citizens, and functioned as if they were program executives no matter which status they were in."[54] Dr. Burns' personal and professional alliances with Ball and Cohen were both close and quite evident. In fact, Myers, in noting the absence in his relationship of "significant discussions with her," suggested unsolicited to the present writer that she would do better to get in touch with Ball and Cohen.[55]

Dr. Burns' friendship with Robert Ball dated from 1953, when she was a member of Secretary of Health, Education and Welfare Oveta Culp Hobby's Committee on Coverage Extension of the Social Security Act and he was the staff advisor for that committee.[56] The Hobby Lobby, as the committee was informally called, was a twelve-person consultant group convened to advance President Eisenhower's

---

[53] Interview with Dr. Burns, 27 May 1984. Ball's role in the Social Security Administration is explained in Chapter IV, footnote 8. Wilbur Cohen held key positions in the Social Security Administration from its inception and was the nation's Secretary of Health, Education, and Welfare in 1968-1969.

[54] Derthick, p. 64.

[55] Robert J. Myers, personal letter to the author. Other sources have also corroborated those friendships.

[56] Interviews with Dr. Burns, 8 August 1982 and 27 May 1984.

interest in expanding Old Age and Survivors Insurance coverage under the Social Security Act. The group operated relatively informally, relying primarily on its discussions and the staff work provided by Ball. It met together regularly over a period of two and one-half months, with full-day meetings each week during most of that time.[57] Dr. Burns was greatly impressed by Ball's knowledge and his quiet, tactful way of making sure that the correct facts were on the table during the group's deliberations. The nature of her participation on the Hobby Lobby must have impressed him in return; a professional camaraderie began which continued until her death in 1985, more than thirty years later. The Hobby Lobby's recommendations were viewed favorably by President Eisenhower and were transmitted to Congress; they became the basis of new legislation enacted soon thereafter, the Social Security Amendments of 1954.

Dr. Burns first knew Wilbur Cohen when they were both employed as staff members of the Committee on Economic Security; she did not, however, have much to do with him at that time.[58] She got to know him well some years later through her friend Loula Dunn, the dynamic former Director of the American Public Welfare Association. Certainly, Cohen was by then familiar with her work; one of her articles was included in a book which he co-edited in 1948.[59] Although the intellectual and political factors cannot be disassociated, it bears noting that Dr. Burns was asked frequently to testify on Social Security Act issues before the House of Representatives' Committee on Ways and Means in the late 1950s. At that time, Wilbur Mills was the

---

[57] Loula Dunn, "Consultants' Report on Extension of OASI," Public Welfare 11 (October 1953): 115.

[58] Eveline M. Burns, oral history interview, 130, Columbia Oral History Collection.

[59] Eveline M. Burns, "Economics Problems in the Provision of Security Against Employment Hazards," in Readings in Social Security, eds. William Haber and Wilbur J. Cohen (New York: Prentice-Hall, 1948).

Committee's powerful Chairman and Cohen was his closest advisor on Social Security program issues.[60] The personal friendship and professional collaboration of Dr. Burns and Wilbur Cohen continued throughout the years. In 1960, she again contributed an article to one of his books.[61] He also shared copies of his work with her, inscribing one volume in 1972 "to my dear friend and colleague, Eve Burns, with my respect and affection."[62]

Dr. Burns' personal involvement with the people who were making or influencing Social Security policies was in large part due to her skills and abilities and to being in the right place at the right time, but it is also likely that her personality was a major factor in opening doors for her ideas. She was interested in people as individuals, expressed herself clearly, and socialized well. She had the ability to mix easily with diverse types of people, to share ideas over drinks, to swap jokes, and generally to put other people at ease. Her intellectual abilities and her skills in dealing with people together helped her to develop and maintain good one-on-one relationships with the people in the inner circles of Social Security throughout the years.

The previous section examined Dr. Burns' policy positions as evidenced in her major writings; this section has considered her relationships with individuals closely involved in Social Security policymaking. One other avenue through which Dr.

---

[60] Interview with Dr. Burns, 27 May 1984.

[61] Eveline M. Burns, "A Salute to Twenty-Five Years of Social Security," in Social Security: Programs, Problems, and Policies, eds. William Haber and Wilbur J. Cohen (Homewood, Ill.: R. D. Irwin, 1960).

[62] The inscription appears in a personal copy of Social Security: Universal or Selective? by Wilbur J. Cohen and Milton Friedman.

Burns worked to influence social change was through her professional affiliations and organizations--as a professor, a public speaker, and in various executive capacities. The following section discusses those activities.

Inside the Profession: Professor, Public Speaker and Organizational Leader

Dr. Burns was a trained economist with social welfare interests and perspective. From her vantage point as a professor, first of economics and later of social welfare, she made use of the opportunities which came her way to have an influence on the ideas and work of others who were, or whom she believed ought to be, concerned with issues of economic security. She also acquired leadership roles in important professional organizations and, in those various capacities, was able to garner additional support for the policy positions in which she believed.

Dr. Burns was on the faculty of Columbia University for a total of thirty-five years, in the Graduate Department of Economics from 1928 to 1942 and in the Graduate School of Social Work from 1946 to 1967. Thus, in all but four years of the 1935 to 1960 time frame covered in this study, she was affiliated in one way or another with the University. Here, as in her one-on-one relationships with people in or near the inner circles of Social Security policymaking as described above, her ability to articulate ideas clearly and well, espousing rational and humane policy positions and showing the logic behind them, combined with her considerable interest and skill in dealing with people, drew others to her way of thinking about social policy issues. These attributes were summed up in the introductory essay of a *festschrift* written and published in her honor by former students and colleagues: "Hers is a knowledge laboriously acquired, widely shared, taught with inspiration, and placed at the service of the community through sustained social action."[63] That knowledge, as it was willingly and inspiredly shared with others through her teaching and social action, contributed to her role in influencing social policy thought and development in the United States. From the perspective of her fellow members in the academic community, her work was unique and to the point. As one professor at Columbia noted,

> massive social expenditures for social purposes, removed from the test of the market, can only be effected through public decisions and through administrative interpretation and the acts of public administrators; <u>this is what social policy, particularly as conceptualized and developed by Burns, is all about</u>.[64]

In the Columbia years, Dr. Burns taught many students about social policy in her classes and seminars and she advised on and directed the writing of numerous dissertations on social insurance and economic security issues. Many of these students went on to government or academic positions, influenced by her ideas and in a position to give them further dissemination through their own work. Among her students were the social economists Blanche Bernstein, Harry Malisoff, Irma Rittenhouse and Sar Levitan. Blanche Bernstein went on to hold posts at the New School for Social Research and the New York State and City Departments of Social Services; Harry Malisoff, at Queens College; Irma Rittenhouse, at the New York State Department of Labor; and Sar Levitan, at George Washington University. Dr. Burns also taught such social work academicians as Winifred Bell, Arthur Katz, Joseph Vigilante and Ronald Dear, all of whom continued to work and write on questions

---

[63] Vera Shlakman, "Eveline M. Burns: Social Economist," in <u>Social Security in International Perspective: Essays in Honor of Eveline M. Burns</u>, ed. Shirley Jenkins (New York: Columbia University Press, 1969), p. 25.

[64] Ibid., p. 6. (Italics mine.)

of social policy after leaving Columbia.[65] These and other students who passed through Dr. Burns' hands continued to draw on their association with her. They cited her works in their own writings, asked her to review and comment on their manuscripts prior to publication, and occasionally co-authored a study or article with her. Students who later joined faculties also incorporated her writings and teachings into their lectures and reading assignments to a subsequent generation of students. As Dr. Burns' writings and teachings became more broadly known, other social welfare professionals who had not studied with her directly were nevertheless so influenced by her ideas that they began to think of themselves as her students. They, too, utilized and transmitted her ideas in the course of their own professional careers.

The academic community also provided Dr. Burns with another way of expanding her network of contacts and potential influence through an informal organization of the heads of doctoral programs of schools of social work which was formed in the 1950s. Since Columbia University and the University of Chicago were the first two schools to offer doctorates in social work, the administrators of those two programs in particular were looked to for leadership. Dr. Burns had been in charge of developing the doctoral program in social work at Columbia and therefore fell naturally into a leadership position in that group. Although it focused more on practical academic matters than on issues of social policy, the group nevertheless represented one more way in which Dr. Burns was able

---

[65] Interviews with Dr. Burns, 8 August 1982 and 24 May 1984. At the time of this research, Winifred Bell was on the faculty at Cleveland State University; Arthur Katz was Executive Director of the Council on Social Work Education; Joseph Vigilante was the Dean of the School of Social Work at Adelphi University; and Ronald Dear was on the faculty at the University of Washington.

to develop a professional audience for her ideas.[66] One of her hopes in reaching out to social work audiences--whether students, faculty members, or practitioners--was that a core group of experts would develop within the social work profession on social policy issues. She felt that the chances for influencing the direction of social policy change would be far greater if there were a constituency to take up the cause of social planning in the area of income security. She knew that professional group advocacy was a potentially powerful addition to the individual advocacy which was being carried out by social welfare professionals such as herself. A core group of social work experts could, she felt, give policy guidance to the rest of the group in order for social workers to provide national leadership on income security and related social policy issues.[67]

In addition to her academic work and affiliations, Dr. Burns attempted to influence the social work profession on issues of policy change through professional organizations, speaking at their meetings and conferences and serving in them in various executive capacities. This activity had its genesis in 1942, after the publication of the National Resources Planning Board report which she had authored. Clarence Bookman, the City Manager of Cincinnati and a member of the National Resources Planning Board, arranged for Dr. Burns to deliver a major paper on her work to the National Conference on Social Welfare. She subsequently received many other invitations to speak at conferences and meetings, and she frequently found herself in the position of explaining social insurance to social workers. She began to come into contact with the leadership of the social work profession; those contacts intensified considerably after she joined the faculty of the Columbia University School of Social Work in 1946. Within the next few years, as she continued to meet and make friends with the established social work

---

[66] Interview with Dr. Burns, 16 January 1984.

[67] Interview with Dr. Burns, 27 May 1984.

leadership at that time, she was elected to membership in the governing board of the National Conference on Social Welfare, a major professional organization whose annual conferences regularly attracted seven or eight thousand participants. In 1955, Dr. Burns became the organization's secretary; in 1956, its first vice-president; and in 1957, its president.[68]

Another professional organization in which Dr. Burns was active in the 1950s was the American Public Welfare Association. She had become friends with Loula Dunn, its Director, who had been a fellow member of Secretary Hobby's Advisory Committee on Coverage Extension of the Social Security Act in 1953. The membership of the American Public Welfare Association included administrators of state and local welfare programs throughout the country. At the request of the American Public Welfare Association's Policy Committee, Dr. Burns prepared a paper for them in 1953, "which was given wide circulation," analyzing current Social Security issues and proposals.[69] She also spoke on Social Security issues at the American Public Welfare Association's Round Table Conference in that same year. Dr Burns subsequently became a member of the Association's Legislative Policy Committee in 1956 and stayed on as a member of that committee for the next twelve years.[70] The Legislative Policy Committee developed policy positions for the full Association. The Association at that time concerned itself with a wide range of income security issues, including Social Security as well as public welfare, and lobbied actively in Washington in pursuit of its policy positions.

---

[68] Interviews with Dr. Burns, 18 June 1983 and 16 January 1984, and personal papers from her files.

[69] Loula Dunn, "Report to the Board of Directors for 1953," Public Welfare 12 (July 1954): 84.

[70] Interview with Dr. Burns, 27 May 1984, and personal papers from her files.

The American Public Welfare Association's legislative objectives, which were set forth as concise statements "no more than four pages long, . . . always [got] into the Congressional Record and . . . [were] widely quoted."[71] According to Arthur Altmeyer, "The American Public Welfare Association had considerable influence on the policies that were adopted" in the Social Security program.[72] Among the legislative policies supported by the American Public Welfare Association and adopted by Congress were the 1954 amendments to the Social Security Act, the product of the Hobby Lobby on which both Dr. Burns and Loula Dunn had participated.[73] It was evident that through professional affiliations and organizations, as well as through scholarly writings and personal relationships, Dr. Burns was exerting leadership and attempting thereby to influence the direction of income security policy change in the United States.

Conflicting Views: Political Opponents and Public Opposition

Although many of the changes advocated by Dr. Burns and others of like mind were enacted over the years, the ideas which she personified were not always popular. She frequently encountered opposition, apathy, or ignorance with respect to Social Security and similar programs. The three points at which she most actively participated, and at which conflicting political and public views were

---

[71] Loula Dunn, oral history interview, 42, Columbia Oral History Collection.

[72] Arthur Altmeyer, oral history interview, 70, Columbia Oral History Collection. Altmeyer was the Chairman of the Social Security Board from 1937-1946 and the Social Security Commissioner from 1946-1953.

[73] Loula Dunn, "Report to the Board of Directors for 1954," Public Welfare 13 (July 1955): 92.

most evident, were in the enactment of the Social Security Act itself, in the reaction to the National Resources Planning Board report, and in the alternative proposals which were being floated at the time of the Hobby Lobby.

The opposition to the Social Security Act in 1935, both in terms of the concept and with respect to its specific content, has been discussed in Chapter III of this study. The authors of the Act were careful to take into account the likely objections of the Supreme Court, the medical profession and organized farmers. The bill as finally written drew protests from business interests on the right, Townsendites and others on the left, and individual experts who objected to the way in which one or another of the programs was designed. Some opponents feared that the programs would be too costly; others retained a staunch faith in federalism and objected to the expanded federal role. The Social Security Act was signed into law in August 1935 and underwent many changes over the years. In general, as proposals for change were introduced and debated, organized labor would take a position in favor of expansion while business groups such as the National Association of Manufacturers and the Chamber of Commerce would join the opposition. The conservative opposition was not to universal coverage, but to higher benefit levels and other program liberalizations.[74]

In contrast to the eventual acceptance of the Social Security bill, the National Resources Planning Board Report of 1942 was relegated to oblivion. It was a far-reaching master plan for post-war economic security, similar to the British Beveridge plan which was released at about the same time.[75] Most of the nation was apathetic to the Report. According to one

[74] Derthick, pp. 132-135.

[75] George Gallup, "American Beveridge Plan Fails to Create Wide Public Stir in U.S.," American Institute of Public Opinion press release, for release April 11 or 12, 1943. (Mimeographed.)

survey,

> in the four weeks since President Roosevelt sent the Resource Board report to Congress, only about one-third of all voters of the nation have heard or read anything about it, and only one in eight is familiar enough with it to be able to cite one or more points dealt with in the report.[76]

Of those people who had heard of the Report, many were vehemently opposed. The Report was decried as representative of foreign ideologies such as Communism and Socialism; it was viewed as paternalistic and a threat to states' rights; it was deemed to be too expensive; and the timing of its release was considered to be distracting in terms of the need for America to keep its attention focused on the war effort.[77] Senator Robert A. Taft of Ohio read an attack on the Report into the Congressional Record.[78] Unfavorable articles and editorials appeared in newspapers in all parts of the country. Dr. Burns spent the better part of a year traveling around the United States, giving speeches and trying to generate broad public support for the Report, but it was finally to no avail. President Roosevelt, concerned about national unity and the demands of the war effort, abolished the National Resources Planning Board as expendable and its plan died with it.[79]

The work product of the Hobby Lobby in 1953 was nowhere near as controversial as the Social Security bill or the National Resources Planning Board Report, but there was one major conflicting view as to what

---

[76] Ibid., p. 1.

[77] Roma K. McNickle, "Editorial Reaction to NRPB Security Report." (Mimeographed, in Dr. Burns' personal files.)

[78] Interview with Dr. Burns, 13 June 1982.

[79] Ibid.

ought to be the Social Security coverage changes at that time. In the fall of 1952, the United States Chamber of Commerce had come out with a policy declaration that called for covering all of the aged under the Social Security program, including both those who met the eligibility criteria and those who did not, with pay-as-you-go financing. The Chamber saw its proposal as a way to have more control over old age and retirement program costs. Program advocates viewed it as a repudiation of contributory, wage-related social insurance and were worried when the new Eisenhower Administration appointed a small group of mostly conservative consultants to study Social Security coverage early in 1953. Organized labor and other program allies protested and succeeded in having the Hobby Lobby enlarged and made more representative.[80] That larger group subsequently presented the Administration with a carefully designed, economically sound set of coverage proposals which it could embrace and send to Congress in place of the less desirable Chamber plan which threatened the underlying principle of a contributory, wage-related social insurance program.

Findings

Dr. Burns made use of multiple avenues and types of activities in attempting to influence the direction of social policy with respect to old age retirement income and the Social Security Act. She produced scholarly writings which explained public policies with respect to old age retirement programs and which set forth the policy changes which she deemed desirable. In the four major books which she wrote between the years of 1935 and 1960 which dealt with Social Security old age retirement policies, she discussed with relative consistency such issues as the extension of coverage, the earnings test, benefit levels and the possible use of general tax revenues to fund part of the costs of the Social Security program. She believed strongly in the policy

---

[80] Derthick, pp. 92-93.

positions which she espoused and, over time, was able to see many of them adopted as part of the overall Social Security program. In the twenty-five years following the passage of the Social Security Act in 1935, coverage was extended to almost all of the major groups of workers who had been excluded in the original legislation. Among the excluded groups had been agricultural and domestic workers, the self-employed, and employees of nonprofit organizations and state and local governments. By 1960, among major worker groups, only self-employed physicians and federal employees already covered by their own retirement system remained outside of the Social Security program. The earnings test, which in 1935 had meant the loss of the entire monthly benefit if a beneficiary had any earnings whatsoever, was modified to exempt older beneficiaries from its application and, for those younger beneficiaries who were still subject to the test, a certain amount of earnings was eventually permitted without benefit reduction and a sliding scale was introduced for reductions due to earnings above that amount. Benefit levels were increased considerably across the board; further, the overall increase was greater at the lower end of the benefit scale. All beneficiaries would henceforth receive more adequate benefits than had previously been the case, but special attention was paid to those who were or would have been receiving the least adequate amounts. The failure to incorporate the use of general tax revenues into the Social Security program in a meaningful way, however, remained a disappointment. There was a brief period during which their use on an emergency basis was authorized; even that authorization was later repealed. Dr. Burns continued to hope, however, that changes in the policy on the use of general revenues would be made at some later time.

In addition to her writings, Dr. Burns was able to press for the policies in which she believed through her personal relationships with people in or near the inner circles of Social Security policymaking. These relationships had come about and were nurtured through a combination of luck, skill, intelligence and other personal attributes, such as the ability to understand and get along well with people. The network of Social Security insiders with whom she had personal, one-on-one relationships grew extensively over the years and encompassed such longstanding, important individuals as Arthur Altmeyer, Robert Myers, Robert Ball, and Wilbur Cohen as well as numerous others both inside and outside of government circles per se.

Finally, Dr. Burns used her professional academic affiliations and her activities with professional social welfare organizations as additional platforms for her views on old age retirement and other income security policies. She gained the attention and respect of students, faculty members and the established social work leadership during her years at Columbia University. She worked at directing the attention of these groups to important social policy issues, particularly in the area of income security and questions related to it. She nurtured a hope that social workers would come to play a much larger role in the development of public income security policies than they had done theretofore and that a core group of social policy experts would grow up within the profession to guide its thinking and help it to exert national leadership on policy matters. It is likely that she envisioned that such a group would have provided important support for many of the same kinds of changes which she espoused. Dr. Burns also turned her energies to providing leadership with respect to existing major professional organizations. Among her many activities, she gave speeches and delivered papers at conferences and meetings, she was a board member and officer of the National Conference on Social Welfare, and she served for many years on the Legislative Policy Committee of the American Public Welfare Association.

In the course of her professional activities, Dr. Burns found herself more than once embroiled in political and public conflict. Two major points at which she was a participant, and at which the views of program advocates won out over conflicting proposals, were the enactment of the Social Security

Act in 1935 and the acceptance of the twelve-member Hobby Lobby proposals in 1953. Not all of her program-related activities, however, met with success; the Report of the National Resources Planning Board in 1942 disappeared from sight without having any perceptible impact on the nation's economic security programs.

In this part of the study, there has been an examination of Burnsian leadership on old age retirement issues in the United States between 1935 and 1960. The historical *zeitgeist* has been described and legislation relating to the Social Security old age retirement program has been traced, particularly with regard to coverage, the earnings test, benefit levels and the use of general revenues. Dr. Burns' activities with respect to old age retirement income policies have been examined from three perspectives: her writings, her one-on-one personal relationships with people in or near the inner circles of Social Security policymaking, and her professional and organizational affiliations. This chapter, Chapter V, has shown in particular how Dr. Burns used her abilities and positions to attempt to influence the direction of social policy with respect to old age retirement income and the Social Security Act. It has also shown how legislation in the twenty-five-year period covered by the present study brought to fruition many of the policy changes which she espoused. Part Three, which follows, sets forth the study conclusions.

PART THREE

CONCLUSIONS

CHAPTER VI

CONCLUSIONS AND IMPLICATIONS

The period from 1935 to 1960 was one in which major policy changes took place in the United States, fueled by economic, demographic, social and political factors which required new policies or contributed to them. Social welfare policies and legislation were affected, for example, by the state of the economy after the Depression, the urban migration of World War II, public sentiment with respect to the aged, and the efforts of well-organized pressure groups on both the left and the right. The major piece of social welfare legislation to come out of that period was the Social Security Act, enacted in 1935 and amended frequently thereafter.

As pointed out in Chapter I of this study, the social work profession has a responsibility to the social welfare institution to help shape the development of social policy. That responsibility is carried out through professional leadership: individuals who can reach down to help shape and guide the policy positions of their interest group and who can reach up in an attempt to influence, directly or indirectly, the decisions of people who have and exercise the policymaking power. Dr. Eveline M. Burns represents a model of professional leadership. This study has examined her efforts to influence Social Security old age retirement policies through her writings and her professional associations, including in the latter category both personal relationships and organizational affiliations. The time frame under consideration was the first quarter-century of the existence of the Social Security program, from its enactment in 1935 to 1960.

The Social Security Act came into being in 1935, one of a bevy of programs instituted as part of President Franklin D. Roosevelt's New Deal. The old age retirement income portions of that act were given particular urgency by the growing pressure on the part of the aged for enactment of a national program which would provide them with income security. One such scheme, advanced by Dr. Francis E. Townsend and his followers, was gaining momentum, but was headed off by the Social Security Act. At the time of its introduction, the proposed Social Security legislation was the object of considerable controversy and opposition, but its supporters prevailed. Its eventual final passage in August of 1935 gave the nation its first nationwide social insurance provisions.

Dr. Burns had been one of the staff members working for the Committee on Economic Security, the Cabinet-level group appointed by Roosevelt to develop the Social Security legislation. After its passage, she immediately began what were to be decades of work garnering support both for the Social Security program and for changes in it. Her position in that regard was clear from the outset:

> It is evident that the Social Security Act, while marking the end of one chapter, is thus only the opening of another. . . . For many years to come . . . the Social Security Act must be the base from which amending and improving operations are conducted.[1]

Four areas to which Dr. Burns paid particular concern in her work over the years, with regard to the Social Security old age retirement income program, were the need for extensions of coverage, the use and structure of the earnings test, improvements in benefit levels, and a hoped-for use of general tax revenues to fund part of the regular operations of the program. She wrote extensively on the issues, spoke to interested audiences at conferences and meetings, took on leadership roles in professional organizations, inculcated graduate students in economics and social work with her ideas on social policy, and developed one-on-one personal

---

[1] Burns, Toward Social Security, p. 235.

relationships with people in or near the inner circles of Social Security policymaking. Through such means, she acquired a vast audience for the Social Security policy agenda--that is, the changes which she deemed desirable and which she therefore believed ought to be made in the Social Security program.

Support for most of the liberalizing changes advocated for the old age retirement program by Dr. Burns and others who thought as she did grew over the years and gave rise to many program improvements, particularly in the 1950s. Between 1935 and 1960, coverage was extended to almost all major groups of workers; the earnings test was modified to apply to fewer beneficiaries and to permit greater retention of earnings; and benefit levels were greatly increased, with the increases proportionately larger at lower levels of earnings. The use of general tax revenues was still not permitted, however, for Social Security old age retirement program purposes.

Dr. Burns' lifelong concern with the need for an expanded and liberalized Social Security program and her efforts in that regard are particularly relevant at present because of the shifting political climate of the 1980s. In the twenty years following after 1960, liberalizing changes continued to be made in the Social Security old age retirement program. The year 1980, however, brought a distinct turning of the tide. The election of Ronald Reagan as President of the United States in 1980 and the advent of his Administration in January 1981 marked the beginning of a new era for Social Security, an era in which advocates had to face up to the realization that the program could be restricted as well as enlarged. Among the deliberalizations of the 1980s were the elimination of some types of dependents' benefits, an increase in the full retirement age, a six-month delay in the automatic cost-of-living adjustment in 1983, and the inclusion of Social Security benefits in the taxable income of some beneficiaries. Further deliberalizations are also likely to be proposed. The need for expert professional leadership on Social Security issues is increasingly important in terms of a renewed national debate over the future shape and existence of the Social Security program.

This study began with the hypotheses that Dr. Burns, in order to try to influence national social policy through the exercise of professional leadership, used her professional positions and associations to gain attention for her views on Social Security old age retirement, to provide and get support for a policy agenda in which she believed, and to advocate for continued legislative and policy change. On the following pages, the three hypotheses are restated and her activities over the years are reviewed to show that she did indeed do all of those things, with considerable success. Her intellectual and other skills, as well as certain of her personal qualities, such as her ability to relate to people, were factors which facilitated her pursuit of professional and public support for her social policy goals. Being in the right place at the right time was also a contributing, if somewhat lesser factor, in her ability to gain attention and support.

The following hypotheses were set forth in Chapter I:

Hypothesis 1. Dr. Burns, through her positions as a highly regarded consultant, professor, and member of professional organizations, was able to gain attention for her views on Social Security old age retirement and used those opportunities to provide a policy agenda on which others in, and outside of, the profession could focus and around which they could coalesce.

Hypothesis 2. Dr. Burns used her associations (advisory committees, schools of social work, professional organizations) as a power base for gathering support for the policy positions which she espoused.

Hypothesis 3. Dr. Burns was a political realist who understood how the legislative process functioned and accepted, but worked for change within, existing government, political and professional structures. She used her influence in the social work profession to urge continued legislative and policy change through the democratic process rather than espousing more radical changes in either policies or methods of attainment.

The first hypothesis was that Dr. Burns was able to gain attention for her views through her professional positions. Dr. Burns spent much of the time between 1935 and 1960 on the Columbia University faculty, first in the Graduate Department of Economics and later in the School of Social Work. Other significant employment in or around the years 1935-1960, from the perspective of this study, included staff work for the Committee on Economic Security and a Research Director position with the National Resources Planning Board. She also acted as a consultant to the Social Security Board for many years during that same time frame. In the course of those jobs, Dr. Burns acquired information about income security policies and issues which she systematically analyzed and developed in her written works. Those works not only explained the issues, but also set forth a Social Security policy agenda and gave it both credibility and visibility. Her four major works dealing with the subject are <u>Toward Social Security</u>; <u>Security, Work, and Relief Policies</u>; <u>The American Social Security System</u>; and <u>Social Security and Public Policy</u>. As her abilities became known and her reputation grew, Dr. Burns also received frequent invitations from both other professionals and the general public to speak about Social Security issues at their organizations' meetings and conferences. These invitations provided her with numerous additional opportunities to raise public consciousness about Social Security program issues and to present her views for consideration.

The second hypothesis was that certain of Dr. Burns' associations provided a power base from which to garner support for preferred policies. The professional respect and reputation which Dr. Burns enjoyed allowed her to move into meaningful organizational and advisory positions in terms of advancing the policy positions which she espoused. She acquired a voice in the policies of the American Association for Old Age (later, Social) Security, an active advocacy organization, first as a member of its National Advisory Committee and subsequently as a Vice-President. She was an articulate member of the Hobby Lobby--a twelve-person consultant group, convened by the Eisenhower Administration, whose recommendations formed the basis of the important Social Security Amendments of 1954. She became active in the affairs of the American Public Welfare Association, particularly as a member of its Legislative Policy Committee. That committee developed income security policy positions for the full Association which were not only heeded by Congress, but which had considerable influence with respect to the legislative policies that Congress adopted.

The third hypothesis was that Dr. Burns worked realistically for continued change within existing government and professional structures. As discussed earlier in this chapter, she expressly regarded the Social Security Act as the basis for future amendments and improvements in the American Social Security system. She worked at developing and maintaining access to the Social Security policymaking structure, establishing solid professional and personal relationships over the years with many of the people who wielded influence in the regular channels of Social Security policymaking--such as John Winant, Arthur Altmeyer, Robert Myers, Wilbur Cohen, and Robert Ball. She testified at Congressional hearings; collaborated on relevant issues with other accepted advocates such as Loula Dunn; and continually impressed upon students, professional colleagues and general audiences the importance of widespread public understanding of the Social Security programs. She wrote, spoke, and taught about the need for a comprehensive and adequate Social Security system which is well-financed and solidly grounded in the nation's values and law. Her work over decades clearly manifests a goal of improved income security through incremental program change.

Dr. Burns' work has clear implications for the social work profession's ability to carry out meaningfully its function of leadership and guidance in the social welfare institution, a function which was explored in Chapter I of the present study. It was pointed out in that chapter that the key to influencing the decisions of policy makers is persuasion, particularly through the skilled practice of partisan analysis. Dr. Burns understood and practiced the art of persuasion and used it to influence the policy ideas and positions of individuals and groups both above and below, in terms of the policymaking hierarchy. She was abetted in that work by her keen analytical ability and a logical, practical mind. Dr. Burns' work and activities provide a model for social welfare professionals with respect to their exercise of leadership on social policy questions and issues. The examination in this study of what she espoused and of how she incorporated policy analysis and advocacy into multiple facets of her work and professional life offers a first-hand picture of how the policy leadership aspect of the professional/institutional relationship can be translated into actual practice. In light of the newly restrictive social policy trends and ideas which gained currency with the election of Ronald Reagan to the United States Presidency in 1980, an understanding of the exercise of professional leadership may well be more important now than at any time in the last fifty years. The need for universal coverage in Social Security is being questioned; benefit levels are being regarded in some quarters as too generous; and the possibility of using general tax revenues for program financing--a particularly pertinent change at a time of a demographically fueled, shrinking ratio of workers to beneficiaries--is increasingly unlikely. Professional leadership must continue, therefore, to be concerned with many of the same issues identified by Dr. Burns in her work. The continuing pursuit of sound social policies for Social Security and other programs faces new obstacles in the wake of the restrictive social attitudes and growing national deficits of the 1980s.

Dr. Burns' work also carries implications for the role which is accorded to social policy expertise by the social work profession. Although her own academic training was in the field of economics, it was noted in Chapter V of this study that she hoped that social work would be the field in which a core group of experts would develop with regard to social policy issues. Clearly, she found in social work the beliefs and values essential to good social policy, but the technical expertise was lacking. She felt strongly that social work education ought to prepare students for careers in social policy, just as it prepares them for other specialized disciplines such as casework and group work. In 1960, speaking on the responsibility of social workers to influence governmental social welfare policy, she pointed out that

> unless social workers have something of a professional nature to contribute in a field that is becoming increasingly technical and which calls for a wide range of knowledge, analytical skills and imaginative intelligence they have no right to expect that consideration will be given to their views, nor can they hope to exert much influence.[2]

In the more than thirty years between that statement by Dr. Burns and the publication of the present study, social work education has not moved decisively toward according social policy a role in the curriculum equivalent to the role of other specializations. If the profession wants to broaden its chances of influencing social policy decision making, it would have to develop a solid, intensive social policy curriculum, together with appropriate field placements and career possibilities for its students. It would have to define and promulgate the study of social policy as both important and practical. Making social policy a significant field

---

[2] Eveline M. Burns, "Responsibility of Social Workers to Influence Governmental Social Welfare Policy," paper delivered at a workshop of the 1960 Alumni Conference of the Columbia University School of Social Work, 9 April 1960, p. 2 (in Dr. Burns' personal files).

of social work study would be a major undertaking on the part of the profession. Not to do so, however, is to risk abdicating a key role of the profession: the shaping and leadership of the social welfare institution in today's society. Dr. Burns' observations on this question in 1960 remain valid as the basis of debate over educational policy as we move further into the 1990s. Here, as with her analysis of the basic themes of Social Security which she first developed and set forth almost immediately after the program's enactment in 1935, her ideas remain part of the fundamental vision of what the institution of social welfare and the profession of social work can and should represent.

The purpose of this study was to examine Dr. Burns' leadership role and her attempts to influence professionals and the public in pursuit of a specific policy agenda. Her approach in the latter regard was precise: "no major analysis is undertaken," wrote one observer and social work professional,

> which does not methodically locate the problem in relation to the economic, demographic, and political forces that surround it, with particular emphasis on points of pressure and change.[3]

With respect to the former, although it was not a part of this study per se, it is nevertheless fitting to end with a tribute to the direct impact of her work.

> Since the American people were thrust into the depression of the 1930s without benefit of protective social measures, first steps in the construction of a social security system were taken in a climate of crisis and emergency. Social policy had to be formulated in the face of a tradition of opposition to governmental intervention in economic matters. And the belief that responsibility for the relief of

---

[3] "Eveline M. Burns: Social Economist," in Jenkins, p. 7.

> want or destitution should be left to lower levels of government, or to voluntary action, reinforced formidable ideological barriers to the expansion of social provision through new social inventions operating outside the market economy. These barriers were eventually breached by the pressure of stark necessity, aided by the contributions of various experts and advocates of social provision, like Dr. Eveline M. Burns.[4]

There is no doubt that Dr. Eveline M. Burns, through her multifaceted professional activities and leadership, left her mark on the field of social welfare policy in the United States. This study, in keeping with its purpose, has described those activities and that leadership which continue to inspire and shape the direction of social policy.

---

[4] Ibid., pp. 3-4.

APPENDIX I

WRITINGS OF EVELINE M. BURNS FROM 1923 THROUGH 1968

Writings of Eveline M. Burns from 1923 through 1968

I. Books

Wages and the State: A Comparative Study of the Problems of State Wage Regulation. London, P. S. King and Son, 1926.

(With A. R. Burns) *The Economic World: A Survey.* London, Oxford University Press, 1927.

Toward Social Security: An Explanation of the Social Security Act and a Survey of the Larger Issues. London, Whittlesey House, and New York, McGraw-Hill, 1936.

British Unemployment Programs, 1920–1938. Report prepared for Committee on Social Security. Washington, D.C., Social Science Research Council, 1941.

Security, Work, and Relief Policies. Report of the Committee on Long-Range Work and Relief Policies to the National Resources Planning Board. (Eveline M. Burns, Director of Research.) Washington, D.C., U.S. Government Printing Office, 1942.

The American Sc .al Security System. Boston, Houghton Mifflin, 1949 (2nd ed. 1951).

The Social Security Act Amendments of 1950: An Appendix to the American Social Security System. Boston, Houghton Mifflin, 1951.

(Editor) *America's Role in International Social Welfare.* By Alva Myrdal et al. New York, Columbia University Press, 1955. (The Florina Lasker Lectures.)

Social Security and Public Policy. New York, McGraw-Hill, 1956. (Published in Spanish as *Seguridad social y acción pública.* Mexico City, Libreros Mexicanos Unidos, 1965. Also published in Arabic.)

(Editor) *Papers and Proceedings of the Conference on Social Policy and Social Work Educaton, Arden House, April 1957.* New York, New York School of Social Work, Columbia University, 1957.

(Editor) *Children's Allowances and the Economic Welfare of Children.* New York, Citizens' Committee for Children, 1968.

II. Pamphlets

Memorandum on "Wall Street Journal" Articles. A Report made for the Bureau of Research and Statistics and the Informational Service of the Social Security Board. Washington, D.C., Bureau of Research and Statistics, 1936. (Memorandum No. 3.)

The Arguments for and against the Old-Age Reserve. Washington, D.C., Social Security Board, 1938.

Discussion and Study Outline on Social Security. Supplement to Joint Statement on Social Security, by the Agriculture, Business, and Labor Committees on National Policy of the National Planning Association. Washington, D.C., The Association, 1944. (Planning Pamphlets, No. 33.)

Comments on the Chamber of Commerce Social Security Proposals. Chicago, American Public Welfare Association, 1953. (Also listed under Articles.)

Private and Social Insurance and the Problem of Social Security. Ottawa, Canadian Welfare Council, 1953. (Also listed under Articles.)

(Editor) *Social Work Education in the Post-Master's Program.* No. 1: *Guiding Principles.* New York, Council on Social Work Education, 1953.

A Research Program for the Social Security Administration. Report of the Advisory Group to the Commissioner of Social Security. (Eveline M. Burns, Chairman.) Washington, D.C., U.S. Government Printing Office, 1961.

Social Policy and the Health Services: The Choices Ahead. New York, American Public Health Association, 1967. (The Bronfman Lectures, No. 6. Also listed under Articles.)

III. Articles

"The French Minimum Wage Act of 1915," *Economica,* III (1923), 236–44.

"The Economics of Family Endowment," *Economica,* V (June 1925), 155–64.

"Productivity and the Theory of Wages," in T. E. Gregory and Hugh Dalton, eds., *London Essays in Economics.* London, G. Routledge, 1927. (Republished: Freeport, N.Y., Books for Libraries Press, 1967.)

"Achievements of the British Pension System," in *Old-Age Security: Proceedings of the Second National Conference.* New York, American Association for Old-Age Security, 1929.

"Statistics and Economic Forecasting," *Journal of the American Statistical Association,* XXIV (1929), 152–63.

"State Pensions and Old-Age Dependency in Great Britain," *Political Science Quarterly,* XLV (1930), 181–213.

"The Social Sciences as Disciplines: I. Great Britain," in *Encyclopedia of the Social Sciences.* 15 vols. New York, Macmillan, 1930–35. Vol. I, pp. 231–47.

"Minimum Wage," in *Encyclopedia of the Social Sciences.* 15 vols. New York, Macmillan, 1930–35. Vol. X, pp. 491–95.

"Does Institutionalism Complement or Compete with Orthodox Economics?" *American Economic Review*, XXI (1931), 80–87.

"The Wider Implications of Social Planning," *The Family*, XIII (1932), 71–74.

"Planning and Unemployment," in Harry W. Laidler, ed., *Socialist Planning and a Socialist Program*. New York, Falcon Press, 1932.

"Misconceptions of European Unemployment Insurance," in *Social Security in the United States: 1933*. New York, American Association for Social Security, 1933.

"Remedies for Maladjustment for Those Who Bear the Brunt of It," *Vassar Quarterly*, July 1933, 253–55.

"The Economics of Unemployment Relief," *American Economic Review Supplement*, XXIII (1933), 31–43.

"Die Nichtlandwirtschaftliche Arbeitslosigkeit in den Vereinigten Staaten, 1930–1932," *Weltwirtschaftliches Archiv*, XXXVII (1933), 529–59.

"Lessons from British and German Experience," in *Social Security in the United States: 1934*. New York, American Association for Social Security, 1934.

"Germany Spends for Recovery," *Today*, February 9, 1935, pp. 14–15.

"Can Social Insurance Provide Social Security?" in *Social Security in the United States: 1935*. New York, American Association for Social Security, 1935.

"Your State and Security," *Survey Graphic*, XXV (1936), 77–79.

"The Lessons of German Experience with Unemployment Relief," in *Lectures on Current Economic Problems*. Washington, D.C., U.S. Department of Agriculture, Graduate School, 1936.

"The Relation of Unemployment Compensation to the Broader Problem of Relief," *Law and Contemporary Problems*, III (1936), 150–56.

"Financial Aspects of the Social Security Act," *American Economic Review*, XXVI (1936), 12–22.

"Basic Principles in Old-Age Security," in *Social Security in the United States: 1936*. New York, American Association for Social Security, 1936.

"Amending the Social Security Act," *Independent Woman*, XVI, No. 4 (April 1937), 108, 118.

"Social Security Act," *Social Work Year Book*, IV (1937), 472–80.

"Social Realities versus Technical Obfuscations," in *Social Security in the United States: 1937*. New York, American Association for Social Security, 1937.

"The Impact of the Social Security Act on the Relief Problem," *National Municipal Review*, XXVII (1938), 13–20, 23.

"Unemployment Compensation in the United States," *International Labour Review*, XXXVII (1938), 584–617.

(With Harry Malisoff) "Administrative Integration of Unemployment and Relief in Great Britain," *Social Service Review*, XII (1938), 374–96.

"Common Sense and Unemployment Compensation," *American Federationist*, XLVI (1939), 248–58.

"Unemployment Insurance," *Social Work Year Book*, V (1939), 449–57.

"An Appraisal of Services for the Unemployed," *Annals of the American Academy of Political and Social Science*, CCII (1939), 45–52.

"Economic Problems in the Provision of Security Against Employment Hazards," *American Economic Review Supplement*, XXX (1940), 68–77. (Reprinted in William Haber and Wilbur J. Cohen, eds., *Readings in Social Security*. New York, Prentice-Hall, 1948.)

"Integration of WPA, Relief, and Unemployment Compensation," in *Proceedings of the Second American Retail Federation Forum*. Washington, D.C., The Federation, 1940.

"Some Fundamental Considerations in Social Security," in *Social Security in the United States: 1940*. New York, American Association for Social Security, 1940.

"Social Security and our Post-War Economy," in *America After the War: Addresses on the General Problem of Full Employment and Minimum Living Standards*. New York, New York University, Institute on Post-War Reconstruction, 1943. (Also in *Journal of Educational Sociology*, XVII [1943], 132–42.)

"The Beveridge Report," *American Economic Review*, XXXIII (1943), 512–33.

"Building for Economic Security—Six Foundation Stones," in Harry W. Laidler, ed., *The Third Freedom: Freedom from Want*. New York, League for Industrial Democracy, 1943. (L.I.D. Pamphlet Series.)

"Toward Security," *American Federationist*, April 1943, pp. 25–27.

"Equal Access to Health" and "Equal Access to Economic Security," in Part I of *National Resources Development Report for 1943*. Washington, D.C., U.S. Government Printing Office, 1943. (Report of National Resources Planning Board.)

"The Security Report of the National Resources Planning Board," in *Proceedings of the National Conference of Social Work, 1943*. New York, Columbia University Press, 1943.

"Planning for Freedom from Want," *Welfare* (Pennsylvania Welfare Conference), IX, No. 4 (Spring Quarter, 1943), 103–110.

"Freedom from Want: The National Resources Planning Board Report," *Survey Midmonthly*, LXXIX (1943), 106–9.

"National Resources Planning Board Proposes Security Program," *National Municipal Review*, XXXII (1943), 232–36.

"Post-War Planning and the Role of Social Security," *Canadian Welfare*, XIX, No. 2 (June 1943), 10–17.

"Security, Work, and Relief Policies," *Bulletin of the New York School of Social Work*, XXXVI, No. 4 (July 1943), 3–11.

"Social Security Plans of the U.S.A.," *Public Affairs* (Institute of Public Affairs, Dalhousie University, Nova Scotia), VI, No. 4 (Summer 1943), 190–94.

"Social Security Planning in the United States," *Agenda*, II (1943), 301–12.

"Economic Opportunity in the Post-War World," *School and College Placement*, III (1943), 26–29.

"Financial Resources of Families," *Journal of Home Economics*, XXXV (1943), 400–401.

"The Place of Social Security in Post-War Planning," *Special Libraries*, XXXIV (1943), 218–24.

"The Rolling Tide of War Migrants," *New York Times Magazine*, May 21, 1944, pp. 14 ff.

"Government and Social Security," *The Nation*, CLIX (1944), 499.

"The American Plan for Social Security: A Comment," *Journal of Educational Sociology*, XVII (1944), 355–58.

"New Perspectives in Social Welfare," *Survey Midmonthly*, LXXX (1944), 15–17.

"Social Insurance in Evolution," *American Economic Review Supplement*, XXXIV (March 1944), 199–211. (Reprinted in Francis S. Doody, ed., *Readings in Labor Economics*. Cambridge, Mass., Addison-Wesley Press, 1950.)

"The Changing Role of Social Work in an Expanding American Economy," *Smith College Studies in Social Work*, XV (1944), 1–14.

"Is Democracy Ready for Social Security?" in *Proceedings of the Ninth Canadian Conference on Social Work*. Winnipeg, The Conference, 1944.

"The Social Services in the Post-War World" and "The Implications of Probable Economic and Social Developments in the Post-War World," in *Educational Planning for Peace: 31st Annual Schoolmen's Week Proceedings*. Philadelphia, University of Pennsylvania, 1944.

Abstract of "The Historical Background, Economic, Social, and Political, of Our System of Social Security," in *Abstracts of Eight Sessions of the Institute on Social Security, April 23 to May 3, 1945*. Washington, D.C., American Council on Education, Committee on Education and Social Security, 1945.

"Reconversion and Its Implications for the Schools of Social Work," *Social Service Review*, XIX, No. 2 (June 1945), 194–200.

"Social Security," in Seymour E. Harris, ed., *Economic Reconstruction*. New York, McGraw-Hill, 1945, pp. 381–96.

"Unemployment Compensation and Socio-Economic Objectives," *Yale Law Journal*, LV (1945), 1–20.

"Social Security Developments in the United States," *The Manchester School* (University of Manchester, England), May 1947, pp. 198–214.

"Social Action and the Professional Social Worker," *The Compass*, XXVIII, No. 4 (May 1947), 37–40.

"The Opportunity of the Private Agency in a Changing World," *Canadian Welfare*, XXIII, No. 5 (October 1947), 3–10. (Also in *Tennessee Public Welfare Record*, August 1948, pp. 134–39.)

"Trends in Public and Private Agency Service," in *Proceedings of the New York State Conference on Social Work*. New York, The Conference, 1948, pp. 18–25.

"Has AAUW a Social Philosophy?" *AAUW Journal*, XLI (1948), 131–36.

"Economic Future of the Family," *Survey Graphic*, XXXVII (1948), 370–72.

"Income Security for the Aged," in *Proceedings of the National Conference of Social Work, 1948*. New York, Columbia University Press, 1949. (Also in *Social Service Review*, XXII [1948], 286–97.)

"Shall We Have Compulsory Health Insurance?—Pro," *The Woman's Press* (YWCA), June 1949, pp. 12, 30–31.

"Economic Factors in Family Life," in *The Family in the Democratic Society*. New York, Columbia University Press, 1949. (Anniversary Papers of the Community Service Society of New York.)

"New Forces in Family Living: Economic Trends," *Journal of Social Casework*, XXX (1949), 50–55.

"How Much Social Welfare Can America Afford?" in *The Social Welfare Forum, 1949: Proceedings of the National Conference of Social Work*. New York, Columbia University Press, 1950. (Also in *Bulletin of the New York School of Social Work*, XLII [1949], 3–18.)

"What Demands Does Social Welfare Make of Those Who Administer It?" in *Proceedings of the Second Annual Conference, sponsored by the Pennsylvania Agency-School Committee on Preparation for Public Social Welfare and the Pennsylvania Association of Colleges and Universities*. Harrisburg, Pa., 1950.

"Trends in our National Economy and their Effect on Public Welfare Planning," *Public Welfare*, VIII (1950), 28–30, 43.

"Our New Social Security," *Survey*, LXXXVI (1950), 429–33.

"An Expanded Role for Social Work," printed with editorial changes as Chapter III of Ernest V. Hollis and Alice L. Taylor, *Social Work Education in the United States*. New York, Columbia University Press, 1951.

"Income During Disability," *Survey*, LXXXVII (1951), 203–5.

"Social Security in a Period of Full Employment," in *Proceedings of the Fourth Annual Meeting of the Industrial Relations Research Association*. Berkeley, Cal., The Association, 1951.

"Further Needs in the Social Insurances," in *The Social Welfare Forum, 1951: Proceedings of the National Conference of Social Work*. New York, Columbia University Press, 1951. (Also in *Social Service Review*, XXV [1951], 283–88, under title "Further Needs in Social Security Legislation in the Field of the Social Insurances.")

"Fifteen Years under the Social Security Act: An Evaluation," in Lois MacDonald, ed., *Current Issues in Social Security*. New York University, Institute of Labor Relations and Social Security, 1951.

"The Future of Social Security," in *No Time To Grow Old.* New York, New York State Joint Legislative Committee on Problems of the Aging, 1951. (Legislative Documents, No. 12.)

"The Doctoral Program: Progress and Problems," in *Social Work Education in the Post-Master's Program.* No. 1: *Guiding Principles.* New York, Council on Social Work Education, 1953. (Also in *Social Service Review,* XXVI [December 1952], 387–98.)

"Private and Social Insurance and the Problem of Social Security," *Canadian Welfare,* XXVIII, No. 7 (February 1953), 5–10, and No. 8 (March 1953), 9–13. (Also listed under Pamphlets.)

"Significant Contemporary Issues in the Expansion and Consolidation of Government Social Security Programs," in *Economic Security for Americans: An Appraisal of the Progress Made from 1900 to 1953.* New York, Columbia University Graduate School of Business, 1954. (American Assembly, 1953.) (Published in Italian as: Punti salienti attuali nella espansione e nel consolidamento dei programmi statali di sicurezza sociale," in *Stato e sicurezza economica negli S.U. D'America: Rivista degli infortuni e delle malattie professionali.* Rome, 1955.)

"Comments on the Chamber of Commerce Social Security Proposals," paper presented at 1953 APWA Round Table Conference, summarized in *Public Welfare,* XII (1954), 4–5. (Also listed under Pamphlets.)

"Wanted: More Thought About Grants-in-Aid," *Social Work Journal,* XXXV (1954), 11–14, 32.

"The New Social Security Proposals," *American Journal of Nursing,* LIV (1954), 460–63.

"The Role of Government in Social Welfare," in *The Social Welfare Forum, 1954: Proceedings of the National Conference of Social Work.* New York, Columbia University Press, 1954. (Also in *Social Work Journal,* XXXV [1954], 95–102.)

"The Financing of Social Welfare," in Cora Kasius, ed., *New Directions in Social Work.* New York, Harper, 1954.

"Current Issues in Social Security," paper presented at 1955 APWA Round Table Conference, summarized in *Public Welfare,* XIV (1956), 45–46.

"Social Security and the American Economy," in *Social Security Kit,* Washington, D.C., American Association of University Women, January 1956.

"Welfare Assistance," in *A Report to the Governor of the State of New York and the Mayor of the City of New York, by the New York State–New York City Fiscal Relations Committee.* New York, The Committee, 1956.

"High Productivity and People's Social Needs," *Public Welfare,* XIV (1956), 154–58.

"Current Economic Trends and Their Impact on Social Policy," *Public Welfare News* (North Carolina Board of Public Welfare), XIX, No.

3 (September 1956), 1–2, 6–7. (Also in *Public Aid in Illinois* [Illinois Public Aid Commission], March 1957, pp. 1–5.)

"Dr. Burns Urges a Broader and More Scientific Approach to Social Work," *Michigan Welfare Journal* (Michigan Welfare League), XV, No. 1 (January 1957), 6–11.

"New Horizons in Social Security," *Social Work*, II, No. 2 (April 1957), 3–7.

"Social Policy and Social Work Education," in *Papers and Proceedings of the Conference on Social Policy and Social Work Education, Arden House, April 1957*. New York, New York School of Social Work, Columbia University, 1957.

"The Problems of Aging," in *Social Studies Kit*, Washington, D.C., American Association of University Women, June 1957.

"A Bigger Role for Volunteers," *Council Woman*, XIX (June 1957), 2–3. (Excerpted in *USIS Feature* [United States Information Service], October 1957, pp. 1–5.)

"New Dimensions in Social Security," *Public Welfare*, XVI (1958), 11–15.

"The Volunteer and the Modern Community," in *The Club Woman and Her Community*. Westchester County Federation of Women's Clubs, 1958.

"Social Welfare Is Our Commitment," presidential address, in *The Social Welfare Forum, 1958: Proceedings of the National Conference on Social Welfare*. New York, Columbia University Press, 1958. (Also in *Public Welfare*, XVI [1958], 147–54.)

"Priorities for Public Welfare," *Social Work*, III, No. 4 (October 1958), 38–44.

"Social Policy and the Social Work Curriculum," Appendix C of Werner W. Boehm, *Objectives of the Social Work Curriculum of the Future*. New York, Council on Social Work Education, 1959.

"The Government's Role in Child and Family Welfare," in Eli Ginsberg, ed., *The Nation's Children*. Vol. III: *Problems and Prospects*. New York, Columbia University Press, 1960. (White House Conference on Children and Youth.)

"Children and Youth in an Affluent Society," *Children*, VII, No. 30 (May-June 1960), 105–9. (Condensation of address at Plenary Session of White House Conference on Children and Youth.)

"A Salute to Twenty-Five Years of Social Security," *Public Welfare*, XVIII (1960), 20–23, 89–90. (Reprinted in William Haber and Wilbur J. Cohen, eds., *Social Security: Programs, Problems, and Policies*. Homewood, Ill., R. D. Irwin, 1960.)

"Social Security Institutions in the Next Decades: An Appraisal of Competing Priorities," in *Proceedings of the Social Security Conference, sponsored by the Labor and Industrial Relations Center, Michigan*

State University, and the Institute of Labor and Industrial Relations, University of Michigan and Wayne State University. East Lansing, Michigan State University Labor and Industrial Relations Center, 1960.

"Social Policy: The Stepchild of the Curriculum," in *Education for Social Work: Proceedings of the Ninth Annual Program Meeting of the Council on Social Work Education.* New York, The Council, 1961.

"Issues in Social Security Financing," in *Social Security in the United States: Lectures Presented by the Chancellor's Committee on the 25th Anniversary of the Social Security Act.* Berkeley, University of California, Institute of Industrial Relations, 1961.

"New Directions in Social Security," in *Fourteenth Annual Conference on Labor.* New York, New York University, 1961.

"The Affluent Society: Its Implications for Health and Welfare," *Welfare* (Pennsylvania Welfare Forum), 1961.

"What's Wrong with Public Welfare?" *Social Service Review,* XXXVI (1962), 111–12.

"New Guidelines for Unemployment Insurance," *Employment Security Review,* XXIX, No. 8 (August 1962), 5–9.

"Unemployment and Workmen's Compensation," *Public Welfare,* XX (1962), 23–26.

"Social Security in Britain—Twenty Years after Beveridge," *Industrial Relations,* II, No. 2 (February 1963), 15–32.

Introduction to Saiyid Zafar Hasan, *Federal Grants and Public Assistance: A Comparative Study of Policies and Programmes in U.S.A. and India.* Allahabad, India, Kitab Mahal, 1963.

"The Functions of Private and of Social Insurance," in *Studi sulle assicurazione, raccolti in occasione del cinquantenario dell'Istituto Nazionale della Assicurazioni.* Milan, A. Giuffrè, 1963. (Also in *Assicurazioni,* XXX [1963], Fasc. 5–6, under title "Le funzioni dell'assicurazione privata e dell'assicurazione sociale.")

"The Basic Undergraduate Social Welfare Course: Its Approach and Content," comment on paper by Richard H. P. Mendes, in *Education for Social Work: Proceedings of the 11th Annual Program Meeting of the Council on Social Work Education.* New York, The Council, 1963.

"Future Social Security Policy and the APWA Leadership Role," *Public Welfare,* XXII (1964), 29–32.

"The Determinants of Policy," in Joseph M. Becker, ed., *In Aid of the Unemployed.* Baltimore, Johns Hopkins Press, 1965.

"The Poor Need Money," *The Nation,* CC (1965), 613–15.

"The Role of Government in Health Services," *Bulletin of the New York Academy of Medicine,* XLI, No. 7 (July 1965), 753–94.

"Needed Changes in Welfare Programs," paper presented at Faculty Seminar on Poverty, Institute of Government and Public Affairs, University of California at Los Angeles, May 1965. Published (without footnotes) in *The Public Interest*, No. 1 (Fall 1965), pp. 82–95, under title "Where Welfare Falls Short." (Reprinted in Bernard J. Frieden and Robert Morris, eds., *Urban Planning and Social Policy*. New York, Basic Books, 1968. Condensed in *Current*, No. 64 (October 1965), under title "Gaps in Our Welfare Programs.")

"New Problems in Social Security," *Canadian Labour*, X, No. 9 (September 1965), 15–19.

"Social Security in Evolution—Toward What?" *Social Service Review*, XXXIX, No. 2 (June 1965), 129–40. (Reprinted in *Canadian Tax Journal*, XIV [1966], 326–36. Shortened version also published in *Proceedings of Annual Conference of Industrial Relations Research Association*, Berkeley, Cal., 1965; in E. Wight Bakke et al., ed., *Unions, Management, and the Public* [3rd ed.], New York, Harcourt, Brace and World, 1968; and in *Monthly Labor Review*, LXXXVIII [1965], under title "Welfare Programs in Evolution.")

"Income Maintenance Policies and Early Retirement," in Juanita M. Kreps, ed., *Technology, Manpower, and Retirement Policy*. Cleveland, World Publishing Co., 1966.

"Tomorrow's Social Needs and Social Work Education," *Journal of Education for Social Work*, II, No. 1 (Spring 1966), 10–20.

"Inventory and Challenge in Services to People," in *Inventory and Challenge: Proceedings of the 20th Anniversary Meeting of the National Social Welfare Assembly*. New York, The Assembly, 1966.

"Some Major Policy Decisions Facing the United States in the Financing and Organization of Health Care," in *New Directions in Public Policy for Health Care: The 1966 Health Conference*. New York, The New York Academy of Medicine, 1966. (Also in *Bulletin of the New York Academy of Medicine*, XLII [1966], 1072–88; *Public Health Reports*, LXXXI [1966], 675–83, under title "Policy Decisions Facing the United States in Financing and Organizing Health Care"; and *American Journal of Nursing*, LXVI [1966], 1580–83, under title "Major Issues in Medicare's Future." Abstract printed in *Hospital Topics*, XLV [1967], 27–28.)

"Social Security in America: The Two Systems—Public and Private," in William Haber, ed., *Labor in a Changing America*. New York, Basic Books, 1966.

"Medicare Begins," *New Society*, VII, No. 196 (June 30, 1966), 18–19.

"Comments on the Health Services Research Papers Conferences," *Milbank Memorial Fund Quarterly*, XLIV (1966), 224–25.

"Social Policy and the Health Services: The Choices Ahead," *American Journal of Public Health*, LVII (1967), 199–212. (Also listed under Pamphlets.)

"The Challenge and the Potential of the Future," in *Comprehensive Health Services for New York City*. Report of the Mayor's Commission on the Delivery of Personal Health Services. New York, The Commission, 1967.

Foreword to Samuel Mencher, *Poor Law to Poverty Program.* Pittsburgh, University of Pittsburgh Press, 1967.

"The Future Course of Public Welfare," in *Position Papers and Major Related Data for the Governor's Conference.* Albany, N.Y., New York State Board of Social Welfare, 1967.

"Childhood Poverty and the Children's Allowance" and "Report on the Conference Proceedings," in Eveline M. Burns, ed., *Children's Allowances and the Economic Welfare of Children.* New York, Citizens' Committee for Children, 1968.

Discussion of "American Social Security in a European Perspective," paper by Gaston V. Rimlinger, in William G. Bowen, et al. eds., *The Princeton Symposium on the American System of Social Insurance: Its Philosophy, Impact, and Future Development.* New York, McGraw-Hill, 1968.

"A Commentary on Gunnar Myrdal's Essay on the Social Sciences and their Impact on Society," in Herman D. Stein, ed., *Social Theory and Social Invention.* Cleveland, Press of Case Western Reserve University, 1968.

"Children's Allowances: A New Scheme for Attacking Poverty," *AAUW Journal*, LXII (1968), 21–23.

"Health Services for All: Is Health Insurance the Answer?" *American Journal of Public Health*, January 1969, Part II, pp. 9–18.

IV. Congressional Testimony

References to Congressional testimony represent a selective listing of some of the major statements presented by Dr. Burns to committees of Congress.

Statement before U.S. Congress, House of Representatives, Committee on Ways and Means, in Economic Security Act: Hearings on H.R. 4120. Washington, D.C., U.S. Government Printing Office, 1935. Pp. 1092–96.

Brief submitted to U.S. Congress, Senate, Committee on Finance, in Economic Security Act: Hearings on S. 1130. Washington, D.C., U.S. Government Printing Office, 1935. Pp. 1006–14.

"The Problems of Unemployment Compensation and Relief." Memorandum prepared for U.S. Congress, Senate, Special Committee to Investigate Unemployment and Relief, November 3, 1937.

Statement before U.S. Congress, Joint Committee on the Economic Report, Subcommittee on Low-Income Families, in Low-Income Families: Hearings Pursuant to Section 5(a) of Public Law 304. Washington, D.C., U.S. Government Printing Office, 1955. Pp. 709–15.

Statement before U.S. Congress, House of Representatives, Committee on Ways and Means, in Social Security Legislation: Hearings on All

Titles of the Social Security Act. Washington, D.C., U.S. Government Printing Office, 1958. Pp. 986–1003.

"Taxation of the Aged: Retirement Income Credit and the Like." Testimony submitted to U.S. Congress, House of Representatives, Committee on Ways and Means, in Tax Revision Compendium. Washington, D.C., U.S. Government Printing Office, 1959. Pp. 551–57.

Statement before U.S. Congress, House of Representatives, Committee on Ways and Means, in Unemployment Compensation: Hearings on Proposed Amendments to the Federal Laws on Unemployment Compensation. Washington, D.C., U.S. Government Printing Office, 1959. Pp. 370–79.

Statement before U.S. Congress, Senate, Committee on Finance, in Social Security Revision: Hearings on H.R. 6000. Washington, D.C., U.S. Government Printing Office, 1963. Pp. 1305–12.

Statement before U.S. Congress, House of Representatives, Committee on Ways and Means, in Medical Care for the Aged: Hearings on H.R. 3920. Washington, D.C., U.S. Government Printing Office, 1964. Pp. 292–313 and 1242.

Statement before U.S. Congress, Joint Economic Committee, Subcommittee on Fiscal Policy, in Income Maintenance Programs, Vol. I. Washington, D.C., U.S. Government Printing Office, 1968. Pp. 347–51 and 362–78.

V. Selected Unpublished Material

These references to unpublished materials have been added to the list of published works because of their particular interest.

"The Integrated Treatment of Unemployment Insurance, Cash Relief, and Emergency Work." Report prepared for Committee on Economic Security, Washington, D.C., 1934.

"Significant Phases of Foreign Experience." Report prepared for Committee on Economic Security, Washington, D.C., 1934.

"Social Security in a Period of Full Employment." Paper presented at the Annual Meeting of the Industrial Relations Research Association, Boston, December 29, 1951.

"Traditions in an Era of Change." Address before 49th Annual Conference, Texas Social Welfare Association, Houston, November 1959.

"The Responsibility of Social Workers to Influence Governmental Social Welfare Policy." Address to Workshop I, 1960 Alumni Conference, New York School of Social Work, New York, April 1960. (Mimeographed.)

"The Changing Role of the American Woman." Paper presented at 75th Anniversary of Flora Stone Mather College, Western Reserve University, March 1963.

"Public and Private Provision for Income Security in Old Age." Paper presented at Sixth International Congress of Gerontology, Copenhagen, August 1963.

"Social Policy and the Economic Outlook." Paper presented at School of Social Work, Ohio State University, February 1964.

"The Economic Security of Children and Youth." Memorandum prepared for President's Task Force on Income Security, August 1964.

"The Guaranteed Minimum Income: Its Effect on Existing Income Security Programs." Paper presented at Conference on the Guaranteed Minimum Income, School of Social Service Administration, University of Chicago, January 1966.

APPENDIX II

PRESIDENTIAL STATEMENT UPON SIGNING THE SOCIAL SECURITY ACT, AUGUST 14, 1935

appendix C

Presidential Statement upon Signing the Social Security Act, August 14, 1935*

Today a hope of many years' standing is in large part fulfilled. The civilization of the past hundred years, with its startling industrial changes, has tended more and more to make life insecure. Young people have come to wonder what would be their lot when they came to old age. The man with a job has wondered how long the job would last.

This social security measure gives at least some protection to 30 millions of our citizens who will reap direct benefits through unemployment compensation, through old-age pensions, and through increased services for the protection of children and the prevention of ill health.

We can never insure 100 percent of the population against 100 percent of the hazards and vicissitudes of life, but we have tried to frame a law which will give some measure of protection to the average citizen and to his family against the loss of a job and against poverty-ridden old age.

This law, too, represents a cornerstone in a structure which is being built but is by no means complete. It is a structure intended to lessen the force of possible future depressions. It will act as a protection to future administrations against the necessity of going deeply into debt to furnish relief to the needy. The law will flatten out the peaks and valleys of deflation and of inflation. It is, in short, a law that will take care of human needs and at the same time provide for the United States an economic structure of vastly greater soundness.

* From "Public Papers and Adresses of Franklin D. Roosevelt, 1935" (Washington, D.C.: U.S. Government Printing Office, 1935).

871

I congratulate all of you ladies and gentlemen, all of you in the Congress, in the executive departments, and all of you who come from private life, and I thank you for your splendid efforts in behalf of this sound, needed, and patriotic legislation.

If the Senate and the House of Representatives in this long and arduous session had done nothing more than pass this bill, the session would be regarded as historic for all time.

APPENDIX III

THE SOCIAL SECURITY ACT: APPROVED, AUGUST 14, 1935 (EXCERPTS)

THE SOCIAL SECURITY ACT

Approved, August 14, 1935

[PUBLIC—NO. 271—74TH CONGRESS]
[II. R. 7260]

AN ACT

To provide for the general welfare by establishing a system of Federal old-age benefits, and by enabling the several States to make more adequate provision for aged persons, blind persons, dependent and crippled children, maternal and child welfare, public health, and the administration of their unemployment compensation laws; to establish a Social Security Board; to raise revenue; and for other purposes.

Be it enacted by the Senate and House of Representatives of the United States of America in Congress assembled,

TITLE I—GRANTS TO STATES FOR OLD-AGE ASSISTANCE

APPROPRIATION

SECTION 1. For the purpose of enabling each State to furnish financial assistance, as far as practicable under the conditions in such State, to aged needy individuals, there is hereby authorized to be appropriated for the fiscal year ending June 30, 1936, the sum of $49,750,000, and there is hereby authorized to be appropriated for each fiscal year thereafter a sum sufficient to carry out the purposes of this title. The sums made available under this section shall be used for making payments to States which have submitted, and had approved by the Social Security Board established by Title VII (hereinafter referred to as the "Board"), State plans for old-age assistance.

STATE OLD-AGE ASSISTANCE PLANS

SEC. 2 (a) A State plan for old-age assistance must (1) provide that it shall be in effect in all political subdivisions of the State, and, if administered by them, be mandatory upon them; (2) provide for financial participation by the State; (3) either provide for the establishment or designation of a single State agency to administer the plan, or provide for the establishment or designation of a single State agency to supervise the administration of the plan; (4) provide for granting to any individual, whose claim for old-age assistance is denied, an opportunity for a fair hearing before such State agency; (5) provide such methods of administration (other than those relating to selection, tenure of office, and compensation of personnel) as are found by the Board to be necessary for the efficient operation of the plan; (6) provide that the State agency will make such reports, in such form and containing such information, as the Board may from time to time find necessary to assure the correctness and verification of such reports; and (7) provide that, if the State or any of its political subdivisions collects from the estate of any recipient of old-age assistance any amount with respect to old-age assistance furnished him under the plan, one-half of the net amount so collected shall be promptly paid to the United States. Any payment so made shall be deposited in the Treasury to the credit of the appropriation for the purposes of this title.

(b) The Board shall approve any plan which fulfills the conditions specified in subsection (a), except that it shall not approve any plan which imposes, as a condition of eligibility for old-age assistance under the plan—

(1) An age requirement of more than sixty-five years, except that the plan may impose, effective until January 1, 1940, an age requirement of as much as seventy years; or

(2) Any residence requirement which excludes any resident of the State who has resided therein five years during the nine years immediately preceding the application for old-age assistance and has resided therein continuously for one year immediately preceding the application; or

(3) Any citizenship requirement which excludes any citizen of the United States.

PAYMENT TO STATES

SEC. 3. (a) From the sums appropriated therefore, the Secretary of the Treasury shall pay to each State which has an approved plan for old-age assistance, for each quarter, beginning with the quarter commencing July 1, 1935, (1) an amount, which shall be used exclusively as old-age assistance, equal to one-half of the total of the sums expended during such quarter as old-age assistance under the State plan with respect to each individual who at the time of such expenditure is sixty-five years of age or older and is not an inmate of a public institution, not counting so much of such expenditure with respect to any individual for any month as exceeds $30 and (2) 5 per centum of such amount, which shall be used for paying the costs of administering the State plan or for old-age assistance, or both, and for no other purpose: *Provided*, That the State plan, in order to be approved by the Board, need not provide for financial participation before July 1, 1937 by the State, in the case of any State which the Board, upon application by the State and after reasonable notice and opportunity for hearing to the State, finds is prevented by its constitution from providing such financial participation. . . .

DEFINITION

SEC. 6. When used in this title the term "old-age assistance" means money payments to aged individuals.

TITLE II—FEDERAL OLD-AGE BENEFITS

OLD-AGE RESERVE ACCOUNT

SECTION 201. (a) There is hereby created an account in the Treasury of the United States to be known as the "Old-Age Reserve Account" hereinafter in this title called the "Account". There is hereby authorized to be appropriated to the Account for each fiscal year, beginning with the fiscal year ending June 30, 1937, an amount sufficient as an annual premium to provide for the payments required under this title, such amount to be determined on a reserve basis in accordance with accepted actuarial principles, and based upon such tables of mortality as the Secretary of the Treasury shall from time to time adopt, and upon an interest rate of 3 per centum per annum compounded annually. The Secretary of the Treasury shall submit annually to the Bureau of the Budget an estimate of the appropriations to be made to the Account. . . .

OLD-AGE BENEFIT PAYMENTS

SEC. 202. (a) Every qualified individual (as defined in section 210) shall be entitled to receive, with respect to the period beginning on the date he attains the age of sixty-five, or on January 1, 1942, whichever is the later, and ending on the date of his death, an old-age benefit (payable as nearly as practicable in equal monthly installments) as follows:

(1) If the total wages (as defined in section 210) determined by the Board to have been paid to him, with respect to employment (as defined in section 210) after December 31, 1936, and before he attained the age of sixty-five, were not more than $3,000, the old-age benefit shall be at a monthly rate of one-half of 1 per centum of such total wages;

(2) If such total wages were more than $3,000, the old-age benefit shall be at a monthly rate equal to the sum of the following:

(A) One-half of 1 per centum of $3,000; plus

(B) One-twelfth of 1 per centum of the amount by which such total wages exceeded $3,000 and did not exceed $45,000; plus

(C) One-twenty-fourth of 1 per centum of the amount by which such total wages exceeded $45,000.

(b) In no case shall the monthly rate computed under subsection (a) exceed $85.

(c) If the Board finds at any time that more or less than the correct amount has theretofore been paid to any individual under this section, then, under regulations made by the Board, proper adjustments shall be made in connection with subsequent payments under this section to the same individual.

(d) Whenever the Board finds that any qualified individual has received wages with respect to regular employment after he attained the age of sixty-five, the old-age benefit payable to such individual shall be reduced, for each calendar month in any part of which such regular employment occurred, by an amount equal to one month's benefit. Such reduction shall be made, under regulations prescribed by the Board, by deductions from one or more payments of old-age benefit to such individual.

PAYMENTS UPON DEATH

SEC. 203. (a) If any individual dies before attaining the age of sixty-five, there shall be paid to his estate an amount equal to 3½ per centum of the total wages determined by the Board to have been paid to him, with respect to employment after December 31, 1936.

(b) If the Board finds that the correct amount of the old-age benefit payable to a qualified individual during his life under section 202 was less than 3½ per centum of the total wages by which such old-age benefit was measurable, then there shall be paid to his estate a sum equal to the amount, if any, by which such 3½ per centum exceeds the amount (whether more or less than the correct amount) paid to him during his life as old-age benefit.

(c) If the Board finds that the total amount paid to a qualified individual under an old-age benefit during his life was less than the correct amount to which he was entitled under section 202, and that the correct amount of such old-age benefit was 3½ per centum or more of the total wages by which such old-age benefit was measurable, then there shall be paid to his estate a sum equal to the amount, if any, by which the correct amount of the old-age benefit exceeds the amount which was so paid to him during his life.

PAYMENTS TO AGED INDIVIDUALS NOT QUALIFIED FOR BENEFITS

SEC. 204. (a) There shall be paid in a lump sum to any individual who, upon attaining the age of sixty-five, is not a qualified individual, an amount equal to 3½ per centum of the total wages determined by the Board to have been paid to him, with respect to employment after December 31, 1936, and before he attained the age of sixty-five.

(b) After any individual becomes entitled to any payment under subsection (a), no other payment shall be made under this title in any manner measured by wages paid to him, except that any part of any payment under subsection (a) which is not paid to him before his death shall be paid to his estate. . . .

OVERPAYMENTS DURING LIFE

SEC. 206. If the Board finds that the total amount paid to a qualified individual under an old-age benefit during his life was more than the correct amount to which he was entitled under section 202, and was 3½ per centum or more of the total wages by which such old-age benefit was measurable, then upon his death there shall be repaid to the United States by his estate the amount, if any, by which such total amount paid to him during his life exceeds whichever of the following is the greater: (1) Such 3½ per centum, or (2) the correct amount to which he was entitled under section 202. . . .

DEFINITIONS

SEC. 210. When used in this title—

(a) The term "wages" means all remuneration for employment, including the cash value of all remuneration paid in any medium other than cash; except that such term shall not include that part of the remuneration which, after remuneration equal to $3,000 has been paid to an individual by an employer with respect to employment during any calendar year, is paid to such individual by such employer with respect to employment during such calendar year.

(b) The term "employment" means any service, of whatever nature, performed within the United States by an employee for his employer, except—

(1) Agricultural labor;

(2) Domestic service in a private home;

(3) Casual labor not in the course of the employer's trade or business;

(4) Service performed as an officer or member of the crew of a vessel documented under the laws of the United States or of any foreign country;

(5) Service performed in the employ of the United States Government or of an instrumentality of the United States;

(6) Service performed in the employ of a State, a political subdivision thereof, or an instrumentality of one or more States or political subdivisions;

(7) Services performed in the employ of a corporation, community chest, fund, or foundation, organized and operated exclusively for religious, charitable, scientific, literary, or educational purposes, or for the prevention of cruelty to children or animals, no part of the net earnings of which inures to the benefit of any private shareholder or individual.

(c) The term "qualified individual" means any individual with respect to whom it appears to the satisfaction of the Board that—

(1) He is at least sixty-five years of age; and

(2) The total amount of wages paid to him, with respect to employment after December 31, 1936, and before he attained the age of sixty-five, was not less than $2,000; and

3 Wages were paid to him, with respect to employment on some five days after December 31, 1936, and before he attained the age of sixty-five, each day being in a different calendar year.

TITLE III—GRANTS TO STATES FOR UNEMPLOYMENT COMPENSATION ADMINISTRATION

APPROPRIATION

SECTION 301. For the purpose of assisting the States in the administration of their unemployment compensation laws, there is hereby authorized to be appropriated, for the fiscal year ending June 30, 1936, the sum of

$4,000,000, and for each fiscal year thereafter the sum of $49,000,000, to be used as hereinafter provided.

PAYMENTS TO STATES

SEC. 302. (a) The Board shall from time to time certify to the Secretary of the Treasury for payment to each State which has an unemployment compensation law approved by the Board under Title IX, such amounts as the Board determines to be necessary for the proper administration of such law during the fiscal year in which such payment is to be made. The board's determination shall be based on (1) the population of the State; (2) an estimate of the number of persons covered by the State law and of the cost of proper administration of such law; and (3) such other factors as the Board finds relevant. The Board shall not certify for payment under this section in any fiscal year a total amount in excess of the amount appropriated therefor for such fiscal year.

(b) Out of the sums appropriated therefor, the Secretary of the Treasury shall, upon receiving a certification under subsection (a), pay, through the Division of Disbursement of the Treasury Department and prior to audit or settlement by the General Accounting Office, to the State agency charged with the administration of such law the amount so certified.

PROVISIONS OF STATE LAWS

SEC. 303. (a) The Board shall make no certification for payment to any State unless it finds that the law of such State, approved by the Board under Title IX, includes provisions for—

(1) Such methods of administration (other than those relating to selection, tenure of office, and compensation of personnel) as are found by the Board to be reasonably calculated to insure full payment of unemployment compensation when due; and

(2) Payment of unemployment compensation solely through public employment offices in the State or such other agencies as the Board may approve; and

(3) Opportunity for a fair hearing, before an impartial tribunal, for all individuals whose claims for unemployment compensation are denied; and

(4) The payment of all money received in the unemployment fund of such State, immediately upon such receipt, to the Secretary of the Treasury to the credit of the Unemployment Trust Fund established by section 904; and

(5) Expenditure of all money requisitioned by the State agency from the Unemployment Trust Fund, in the payment of unemployment compensation, exclusive of expenses of administration; and

(6) The making of such reports, in such form and containing such information, as the Board may from time to time require, and compliance with such provisions as the Board may from time to time find necessary to assure the correctness and verification of such reports; and

(7) Making available upon request to any agency of the United States charged with the administration of public works or assistance through

public employment, the name, address, ordinary occupation and employment status of each recipient of unemployment compensation, and a statement of such recipient's rights to further compensation under such law.

(b) Whenever the Board, after reasonable notice and opportunity for hearing to the State agency charged with the administration of the State law, finds that in the administration of the law there is—

(1) a denial, in a substantial number of cases, of unemployment compensation to individuals entitled thereto under such law; or

(2) a failure to comply substantially with any provision specified in subsection (a);

the Board shall notify such State agency that further payments will not be made to the State until the Board is satisfied that there is no longer any such denial or failure to comply. Until it is so satisfied, it shall make no further certification to the Secretary of the Treasury with respect to such State.

TITLE IV—GRANTS TO STATES FOR AID TO DEPENDENT CHILDREN

APPROPRIATION

SECTION 401. For the purpose of enabling each State to furnish financial assistance, as far as practicable under the conditions in such State, to needy dependent children, there is hereby authorized to be appropriated for the fiscal year ending June 30, 1936, the sum of $24,750,000, and there is hereby authorized to be appropriated for each fiscal year thereafter a sum sufficient to carry out the purposes of this title. The sums made available under this section shall be used for making payments to States which have submitted, and had approved by the Board, State plans for aid to dependent children.

STATE PLANS FOR AID TO DEPENDENT CHILDREN

SEC. 402. (a) A State plan for aid to dependent children must (1) provide that it shall be in effect in all political subdivisions of the State, and, if administered by them, be mandatory upon them; (2) provide for financial participation by the State; (3) either provide for the establishment or designation of a single State agency to administer the plan, or provide for the establishment or designation of a single State agency to supervise the administration of the plan; (4) provide for granting to any individual, whose claim with respect to aid to a dependent child is denied, an opportunity for a fair hearing before such State agency; (5) provide such methods of administration (other than those relating to selection, tenure of office, and compensation of personnel) as are found by the Board to be necessary for the efficient operation of the plan; and (6) provide that the State agency will make such reports, in such form and containing such information, as the Board may from time to time require, and comply with such provisions as the Board may from time to time find necessary to assure the correctness and verification of such reports.

(b) The Board shall approve any plan which fulfills the conditions specified in subsection (a), except that it shall not approve any plan which imposes as a condition of eligibility for aid to dependent children, a residence requirement which denies aid with respect to any child residing in the State (1) who has resided in the State for one year immediately preceding the application for such aid, or (2) who was born within the State within one year immediately preceding the application, if its mother has resided in the State for one year immediately preceding the birth.

PAYMENT TO STATES

SEC. 403. (a) From the sums appropriated therefor, the Secretary of the Treasury shall pay to each State which has an approved plan for aid to dependent children, for each quarter, beginning with the quarter commencing July 1, 1935, an amount, which shall be used exclusively for carrying out the State plan, equal to one-third of the total of the sums expended during such quarter under such plan, not counting so much of such expenditure with respect to any dependent child for any month as exceeds $18, or if there is more than one dependent child in the same home, as exceeds $18 for any month with respect to one such dependent child and $12 for such month with respect to each of the other dependent children. . . .

DEFINITIONS

SEC. 406. When used in this title—

(a) The term "dependent child" means a child under the age of sixteen who has been deprived of parental support or care by reason of the death, continued absence from the home, or physical or mental incapacity of a parent, and who is living with his father, mother, grandfather, grandmother, brother, sister, stepfather, stepmother, stepbrother, stepsister, uncle, or aunt, in a place of residence maintained by one or more of such relatives as his or their own home;

(b) The term "aid to dependent children" means money payments with respect to a dependent child or dependent children.

TITLE V—GRANTS TO STATES FOR MATERNAL AND CHILD WELFARE

PART 1—MATERNAL AND CHILD HEALTH SERVICES

APPROPRIATION

SECTION 501. For the purpose of enabling each State to extend and improve, as far as practicable under the conditions in such State, services for promoting the health of mothers and children, especially in rural areas and in areas suffering from severe economic distress, there is herby authorized to be appropriated for each fiscal year, beginning with the fiscal year ending June 30, 1936, the sum of $3,800,000. The sums made available under this section shall be used for making payments to States which have submitted, and had approved by the Chief of the Children's Bureau, State plans for such services.

ALLOTMENTS TO STATES

SEC. 502. (a) Out of the sums appropriated pursuant to section 501 for each fiscal year the Secretary of Labor shall allot to each State $20,000, and such part of $1,800,000 as he finds that the number of live births in such State bore to the total number of live births in the United States, in the latest calendar year for which the Bureau of the Census has available statistics.

(b) Out of the sums appropriated pursuant to section 501 for each fiscal year the Secretary of Labor shall allot to the States $980,000 (in addition to the allotments made under subsection (a), according to the financial need of each State for assistance in carrying out its State plan, as determined by him after taking into consideration the number of live births in such State.

(c) The amount of any allotment to a State under subsection (a) for any fiscal year remaining unpaid to such State at the end of such fiscal year shall be available for payment to such State under section 504 until the end of the second succeeding fiscal year. No payment to a State under section 504 shall be made out of its allotment for any fiscal year until its allotment for the preceding fiscal year has been exhausted or has ceased to be available.

APPROVAL OF STATE PLANS

SEC. 503. (a) A State plan for maternal and child-health services must (1) provide for financial participation by the State; (2) provide for the administration of the plan by the State health agency or the supervision of the administration of the plan by the State health agency; (3) provide such methods of administration (other than those relating to selection, tenure of office, and compensation of personnel) as are necessary for the efficient operation of the plan; (4) provide that the State health agency will make such reports, in such form and containing such information, as the Secretary of Labor may from time to time find necessary to assure the correctness and verification of such reports; (5) provide for the extension and improvement of local maternal and child-health services administered by local child-health units; (6) provide for cooperation with medical, nursing, and welfare groups and organization; and (7) provide for the development of demonstration services in needy areas and among groups in special need.

(b) The Chief of the Children's Bureau shall approve any plan which fulfills the conditions specified in subsection (a) and shall thereupon notify the Secretary of Labor and the State health agency of his approval . . . .

PART 2—SERVICES FOR CRIPPLED CHILDREN

APPROPRIATION

SEC. 511. For the purpose of enabling each State to extend and improve (especially in rural areas and in areas suffering from severe economic distress), as far as practicable under the conditions in such State, services for locating crippled children, and for providing medical, surgical, corrective, and other services and care, and facilities for diagnosis, hospitalization, and aftercare, for children who are crippled or who are suffering from conditions which lead to crippling, there is hereby authorized to be appropriated for each fiscal year, beginning with the fiscal year ending June 30, 1936, the sum of $2,850,000. The sums made available under this section shall be used for making payments to States which have submitted, and had approved by the Chief of the Children's Bureau, State plans for such services.

ALLOTMENTS TO STATES

SEC. 512. (a) Out of the sums appropriated pursuant to section 511 for each fiscal year the Secretary of Labor shall allot to each State $20,000, and the remainder to the States according to the need of each State as determined by him after taking into consideration the number of crippled children in such State in need of the services referred to in section 511 and the cost of furnishing such services to them.

(b) The amount of any allotment to a State under subsection (a) for any fiscal year remaining unpaid to such State at the end of such fiscal year shall be available for payment to such State under section 514 until the end of the second succeeding fiscal year. No payment to a State under section 514 shall be made out of its allotment for any fiscal year until its allotment for the preceding fiscal year has been exhausted or has ceased to be available.

APPROVAL OF STATE PLANS

SEC. 513. (a) A State plan for sevices for crippled children must (1) provide for financial participation by the State; (2) provide for the administration of the plan by a State agency or the supervision of the administration of the plan by a State agency; (3) provide such methods of administration (other than those relating to selection, tenure of office, and compensation of personnel) as are necessary for the efficient operation of the plan; (4) provide that the State agency will make such reports, in such form and containing such information, as the Secretary of Labor may from time to time require, and comply with such provisions as he may from time to time find necessary to assure the correctness and verification of such reports; (5) provide for carrying out the purposes specified in section 511; and (6) provide for cooperation with medical, health, nursing, and welfare groups and organizations and with any agency in such State charged with administering State laws providing for vocational rehabilitation of physically handicapped children.

(b) The Chief of the Children's Bureau shall approve any plan which fulfills the conditions specified in subsection (a) and shall thereupon notify the Secretary of Labor and the State health agency of his approval. . . .

PART 3—CHILD-WELFARE SERVICES

SEC. 521. (a) For the purpose of enabling the United States, through the Children's Bureau, to cooperate with State public-welfare agencies in establishing, extending, and strengthening, especially in predominantly rural areas, public-welfare services (hereinafter in this section referred to as "child-welfare services") for the protection and care of homeless, dependent, and neglected children, and children in danger of becoming delinquent, there is hereby authorized to be appropriated for each fiscal year, beginning with the fiscal year ending June 30, 1936, the sum of $1,500,000. Such amount shall be allotted by the Secretary of Labor for use by cooperating State public-welfare agencies on the basis of plans developed jointly by the State agency and the Children's Bureau, to each State, $10,000, and the remainder to each State on the basis of such plans, not to exceed such part of the remainder as the rural population of such State bears to the total rural population of the United States. The amount so allotted shall be expended for payment of part of the cost of district, county or other local child-welfare services in areas predominantly rural, and for developing State services for the encouragement and assistance of adequate methods of community child-welfare organization in areas predominantly rural and other areas of special need. The amount of any allotment to a State under this section for any fiscal year remaining unpaid to such State at the end of such fiscal year shall be available for payment to such State under this section until the end of the second succeeding fiscal year. No payment to a State under this section shall be made out of its allotment for any fiscal year until its allotment for the preceding fiscal year has been exhausted or has ceased to be available . . . .

Part 4—Vocational Rehabilitation

Sec. 531. (a) In order to enable the United States to cooperate with the States and Hawaii in extending and strengthening their programs of vocational rehabilitation of the physically disabled, and to continue to carry out the provisions and purposes of the Act entitled "An Act to provide for the promotion of vocational rehabilitation of persons disabled in industry or otherwise and their return to civil employment," approved June 2, 1920, as amended (U.S.C., title 29, ch. 4; U.S.C., Supp. VII, title 29, secs. 31, 32, 34, 35, 37, 39, and 40), there is hereby authorized to be appropriated for the fiscal years ending June 30, 1936, and June 30, 1937, the sum of $841,000 for each fiscal year in addition to the amount of the existing authorization, and for each fiscal year thereafter the sum of $1,938,000. Of the sums appropriated pursuant to such authorization for each fiscal year, $5,000 shall be apportioned to the Territory of Hawaii and the remainder shall be apportioned among the several States in the manner provided in such Act of June 2, 1920, unamended. . . .

Part 5—Administration

Sec. 541. (a) There is hereby authorized to be appropriated for the fiscal year ending June 30, 1936, the sum of $425,000, for all necessary expenses of the Children's Bureau in administering the provisions of this title, except section 531.

(b) The Children's Bureau shall make such studies and investigations as will promote the efficient administration of this title, except section 531.

(c) The Secretary of Labor shall include in his annual report to Congress a full account of the administration of this title, except section 531. . . .

TITLE X—GRANTS TO STATES FOR AID TO THE BLIND

APPROPRIATION

SECTION 1001. For the purpose of enabling each State to furnish financial assistance, as far as practicable under the conditions in such State, to needy individuals who are blind, there is hereby authorized to be appropriated for the fiscal year ending June 30, 1936, the sum of $3,000,000, and there is hereby authorized to be appropriated for each fiscal year thereafter a sum sufficient to carry out the purposes of this title. The sums made available under this section shall be used for making payments to States which have submitted, and had approved by the Social Security Board, State plans for aid to the blind.

STATE PLANS FOR AID TO THE BLIND

SEC. 1002. (a) A State plan for aid to the blind must (1) provide that it shall be in effect in all political subdivisions of the State, and if administered by them, be mandatory upon them; (2) provide for financial participation by the State; (3) either provide for the establishment or designation of a single State agency to adminster the plan, or provide for the establishment or designation of a single State agency to supervise the administration of the plan; (4) provide for granting to any individual, whose claim for aid is denied, an opportunity for a fair hearing before such State agency; (5) provide such methods of administration (other than those relating to selection, tenure of office, and compensation of personnel) as are found by the Board to be necessary for the efficient operation of the plan; (6) provide that the State agency will make such reports, in such form and containing such information, as the Board may from time to time require, and comply with such provisions as the Board may from time to time find necessary to assure the correctness and verification of such reports; and (7) provide that no aid will be furnished any individual under the plan with respect to which he is receiving old-age assistance under the State plan approved under section 2 of this Act.

(b) The Board shall approve any plan which fulfills the conditions specified in subsection (a), except that it shall not approve any plan which imposes, as a condition of eligibility for aid to the blind under the plan—

(1) Any residence requirement which excludes any resident of the State who has resided therein five years during the nine years immediately preceding the application for aid and has resided therein continuously for one year immediately preceding the application; or

(2) Any citizenship requirement which excludes any citizen of the United States.

PAYMENT TO STATES

SEC. 1003. (a) From the sums appropriated therefor, the Secretary of the Treasury shall pay to each State which has an approved plan for aid to the blind, for each quarter, beginning with the quarter commencing July 1, 1935, (1) an amount, which shall be used exclusively as aid to the blind, equal to one-half of the total of the sums expended during such quarter as aid to the blind under the State plan with respect to each individual who is blind and is not an inmate of a public institution, not counting so much of such expenditure with respect to any individual for any month as exceeds $30, and (2) 5 per centum of such amount, which shall be used for paying the costs of administering the State plan or for aid to the blind, or both, and for no other purpose. . . .

SHORT TITLE

SEC. 1105. This Act may be cited as the "Social Security Act."
Approved, August 14, 1935.

APPENDIX IV

SUMMARY OF PROVISIONS OF THE FEDERAL SOCIAL SECURITY ACT RELATING TO FEDERAL OLD-AGE BENEFITS AND FEDERAL EMPLOYMENT TAXES

Appendix

SUMMARY OF PROVISIONS OF THE FEDERAL SOCIAL SECURITY ACT RELATING TO FEDERAL OLD-AGE BENEFITS AND FEDERAL EMPLOYMENT TAXES

(Public No. 271, 74th Cong. [H. R. 7260]; Approved Aug. 14, 1935)

Issued by the Social Security Board

Federal Old-age Benefits (Title II)

Coverage (Sec. 210*b*)

Old-age benefits are to be paid to all employees based upon wages received in employment in any service performed within the United States, Alaska and Hawaii except:

1. Agricultural labor,
2. Domestic service in a private home,
3. Casual labor not in the course of employer's trade or business,
4. Officers or members of the crew of a vessel documented under the laws of the United States or of any foreign country,
5. Employees of the United States Government,
6. Employees of a state or political subdivision,
7. Employees of nonprofit institutions operated exclusively for religious, charitable, scientific,

literary, or educational purposes, or for the prevention of cruelty to children or animals,

8. Employees of a carrier as defined in Railroad Retirement Act of 1935 (Public No. 399, 74th Cong. [H.R. 8651]).

Conditions to Qualify for Receipt of Old-age Benefits (Sec. 210c)

1. At least sixty-five years of age,
2. Not less than $2,000 total wages received after December 31, 1936, and before age of sixty-five,
3. Wages were paid to individual on some day in each of five years after December 31, 1936, and before age of sixty-five.

Old-age Benefit Payments (Sec. 202)

1. Date first payable—January 1, 1942.
2. The amount of the monthly benefits payable is determined as follows:

Total wages received after December 31, 1936, and prior to age sixty-five, in covered employments		Per cent of total wages paid as monthly benefit
Not counting wages in excess of $3,000 annually.		
First	$ 3,000	1/2 per cent
Next	42,000	1/12 per cent
All over	45,000	1/24 per cent

Federal Administration

Old-age Reserve Account in the U. S. Treasury. The Secretary of the Treasury submits annual estimate to Budget of appropriation to be made to account; and invests funds which draw interest at 3 per cent (Sec. 201).

Social Security Board determines the qualifications of the individual and amount of benefits payable (Sec. 202*a*); certifies to Treasury persons entitled to payments (Sec. 207).

Federal Taxes with Respect to Employment (Title VIII)

Coverage (Sec. 811*b*)

Federal taxes are to be paid by all employers and employees based on wages received in employment in any service performed within the United States, Alaska and Hawaii except:

1. Agricultural labor,
2. Domestic service in a private home,
3. Casual labor not in the course of employer's trade or business,
4. An individual who has attained sixty-five years,
5. Officers or members of the crew of a vessel documented under the laws of the United States or of any foreign country,
6. Employees of the United States government,
7. Employees of a state or a political subdivision,
8. Employees of nonprofit institutions operated exclusively for religious, charitable, scientific, literary, or educational purposes, or for the prevention of cruelty to children or animals,

APPENDIX

9. Employees of a carrier as defined in (Public No. 400, 74th Cong. [H.R. 8652]).

Rates of Taxes

Taxes assessed on wages not counting in excess of $3,000 annually paid any individual (Sec. 811*a*).

INCOME TAX ON WAGES OF EMPLOYEES (SEC. 801)

Calendar year	Tax
1937, 1938, and 1939	1 per cent
1940, 1941, and 1942	1½ per cent
1943, 1944, and 1945	2 per cent
1946, 1947, and 1948	2½ per cent
1949 and thereafter	3 per cent

Income tax on employee collected by employer by deducting the tax from wages (Sec. 802*a*). But such a tax not to be allowed as a deduction in computing net income for Income Tax purposes (Sec. 803).

EXCISE TAX ON WAGES PAID BY EMPLOYERS (SEC. 804)

Calendar year	Tax
1937, 1938, and 1939	1 per cent
1940, 1941, and 1942	1½ per cent
1943, 1944, and 1945	2 per cent
1946, 1947, and 1948	2½ per cent
1949 and thereafter	3 per cent

APPENDIX

3. Illustrative benefits are as follows:

Average monthly salary	Years of employment			
	10	20	30	40
$ 50	$17.50	$22.50	$27.50	$32.50
100	22.50	32.50	42.50	51.25
150	27.50	42.50	53.75	61.25
200	32.50	51.25	61.25	71.25
250	37.50	56.25	68.75	81.25

Minimum monthly benefit, $10; maximum, $85.

4. Non-qualified individuals upon reaching age of sixty-five are paid a lump sum equal to 3½ per cent of the total wages paid after December 31, 1936, and before the attainment of age sixty-five (Sec. 204).
5. Upon death of individual before age of sixty-five, his estate receives payment equal to 3½ per cent of his total wages received after December 31, 1936; if he dies after age of sixty-five, his estate receives the same amount less any benefits paid to him during his lifetime (Sec. 208).
6. Payment of benefit withheld for each month in which a qualified individual who has attained age sixty-five received wages for regular employment (Sec. 202d).
7. Payments not subject to assignment or other legal process (Sec. 208).

Federal Administration

Taxes collected by Bureau of Internal Revenue under direction of Secretary of Treasury and paid into United States Treasury as internal-revenue collections (Sec. 807*a*). Commissioner of Internal Revenue with approval of Secretary of Treasury makes rules for enforcement of title (Sec. 808).

Taxes collected in such manner, at such time, and under such conditions (either by making and filing returns or by stamps, coupons, tickets, books, or other reasonable devices or methods) as may be prescribed by the Commissioner of Internal Revenue, who furnishes to the Postmaster General a suitable quantity to be kept at post offices. The Postmaster General at least once a month transfers to Treasury as internal-revenue collections all receipts so deposited (Sec. 809).

SUMMARY OF PROVISIONS OF THE FEDERAL SOCIAL SECURITY ACT RELATING TO UNEMPLOYMENT COMPENSATION

(Public No. 271, 74th Cong. [H.R. 7260]; Approved Aug. 14, 1935)

Issued by the Social Security Board

To be administered by the Social Security Board established by Title VII of the Act

FEDERAL GRANTS TO STATES FOR ADMINISTRATION OF UNEMPLOYMENT COMPENSATION (TITLE III)

Amount of Federal Appropriation Authorized (Sec. 301)

Fiscal year ending June 30, 1936—$ 4,000,000.
Fiscal years thereafter — 49,000,000.

Amount of Grant to Each State (Sec. 302*a*)

Such amount granted from time to time as the Social Security Board determines to be necessary for the proper administration of the state law during the fiscal year in which payment is to be made, taking into account:

1. Population of the state;
2. Number of persons covered by the state law and the cost of proper administration thereof;
3. Such other factors as the Social Security Board finds relevant.

The Secretary of the Treasury upon receipt of certification of the Social Security Board shall pay prior to audit or settlement by the General Accounting Office the amount certified to the state agency charged with the administration of the law.

The Social Security Board shall not certify payments in excess of the amount appropriated for any fiscal year.

State Matching Required

None.

Required Provisions of State Unemployment Compensation Administration for receipt of Federal Grants (Sec. 303*a*)

1. Approval of state law by Social Security Board under title IX.

2. "Such methods of administration (other than those relating to selection, tenure of office, and compensation of personnel) as are found by the Board to be reasonably calculated to insure full payment of unemployment compensation when due; and

3. "Payment of unemployment compensation solely through public employment offices in the state or such other agencies as the Board may approve; and

4. "Opportunity for a fair hearing, before an impartial tribunal, for all individuals whose claims for unemployment compensation are denied; and

5. "The payment of all money received in the unemployment fund of such state, immediately upon such receipt, to the Secretary of the Treasury to the credit of the Unemployment Trust Fund established by section 904; and

6. "Expenditure of all money requisitioned by the state agency from the Unemployment Trust Fund, in the payment of unemployment compensation, exclusive of expenses of administration; and

APPENDIX

7. "The making of such reports, in such form and containing such information, as the Board may from time to time require, and compliance with such provisions as the Board may from time to time find necessary to assure the correctness and verification of such reports;" and

8. Making available upon request to any federal agency administering public works or assistance through public employment, the name, address, occupation, employment status and rights to further compensation of each recipient of unemployment compensation.

Suspension of Grants (Sec. 303*b*)

If the Social Security Board finds, after reasonable notice and opportunity for hearing to the state agency, either (1) that a substantial number of persons entitled to compensation are being denied compensation, or (2) that the state has failed to comply substantially with the provisions required in section 303*a*, the Board shall notify such state agency that further payment will not be made until the Board is satisfied that there is no longer any such denial or failure to comply.

Federal Tax upon Employers of Eight or More Employees (Title IX)

Coverage of Federal Tax (Sec. 907)

Employers of eight or more individuals employed on each of some 20 days in year, each day being in a different calendar week, in employments performed within the United States, except the following employments:

1. Agricultural labor;
2. Domestic service in a private home;

3. Officer or member of the crew of a vessel on the navigable waters of the United States.

4. Individual in the employ of son, daughter, or spouse; child under 21 years in employ of his parent;

5. Public employees—federal, state and local;

6. Employees of nonprofit institutions operated exclusively for religious, charitable, scientific, literary, or educational purposes, or for the prevention of cruelty to children or animals.

Rate of Tax on Employers (Sec. 901)

1 per cent of wages paid in 1936; 2 per cent in 1937; 3 per cent thereafter.

Credit Allowed for Payments under State Unemployment Compensation Law

1. Not to exceed 90 per cent of federal tax. (Sec. 902)

2. After 1937 additional credit is also allowable to any employer who because of favorable employment experience or adequate reserves is permitted by the state law to reduce his payments, subject to the following conditions (Sec. 910):

(a) If the employer contributes to a state pooled fund, the lower rate is based upon not less than three years' compensation experience.

(b) If the employer contributes to a guaranteed employment account, the lower rate is permitted only if the guaranty was fulfilled during the preceding year and the account amounts to not less than 7½ per cent of total wages paid during the preceding calendar year.

(c) If the employer contributes to a separate reserve account, the lower rate is permitted only if (1) compensation has been payable from the account throughout the preceding calendar year, (2) the account amounts to not less than five times the largest amount of compensation paid during any one of the three preceding calendar years, and (3) such account amounts to 7½ per cent of the wages paid during the preceding year.

Required Provisions of State Unemployment Compensation Law for Allowance of Credit (Sec. 903*a*)

1. All compensation to be paid through public employment offices in the state or such other agencies as the Board may approve;

2. No compensation to be payable until after two years after contributions first required;

3. State unemployment fund to be deposited with the Unemployment Trust Fund of the U. S. Treasury;

4. Money withdrawn from the Unemployment Trust Fund to be used solely for unemployment compensation, exclusive of administrative expenses;

5. Compensation not to be denied any eligible individual for refusal to accept work if (a) the position vacant is due directly to a strike, lockout, or labor dispute, (b) the wages, hours, or conditions of work are substantially less favorable to the individual than those prevailing in the locality, or (c) if the individual would be required to join a company union or to resign from, or refrain from joining a bona fide labor organization;

6. State must retain the right to repeal or amend its law.

Revocation of Approval of State Plans (Sec. 903*b*)

The Social Security Board may, at end of any year after reasonable notice and opportunity for hearing, refuse to certify state whose plan has been previously approved in case the state law has been changed so that it no longer contains the above conditions, or if the state has failed to comply substantially with these conditions. If at any time the Board has reason to believe a state law may not be certified it shall promptly notify the Governor.

Unemployment Trust Fund (Sec. 904)

All moneys received in the state unemployment fund must be deposited in the Unemployment Trust Fund maintained by the United States Treasury, subject to requisition of the state. These funds are invested by the Treasury and bear interest at the average rate paid by the United States upon all interest-bearing obligations. A separate account is maintained for each state.

Interstate Commerce (Sec. 906)

No person required by state law to make payments to an unemployment compensation fund shall be relieved on the ground that he is engaged in interstate commerce, or that the state law does not distinguish between employees engaged in interstate and intrastate commerce.

Summary of Provisions of the Social Security Act Relating to Federal Grants to States

SUMMARY OF PROVISIONS OF THE SOCIAL SECURITY

(Public No. 271, 74th Cong.

<table>
<tr><th>Provision</th><th>Old-age assistance (Secs. 1–6)</th><th>Aid to the blind (Secs. 1001–1006)</th><th>Aid to dependent children (Secs. 401–406)</th></tr>
<tr><td>Conditions for approval of state plan.</td><td colspan="3">1. A state plan (for each type of assistance, aid, or service) must be federal administrative agency for approval.
For old-age assistance, aid to the blind, and aid to dependent children, each of the plans must be state-wide, and, if administered by political subdivisions, must be mandatory upon them.
2. Financial participation by the state must be provided in the state service).</td></tr>
<tr><td></td><td>A state old-age assistance plan need not provide state financial participation before July 1, 1937, where the Board finds the state is so prevented by its constitution.</td><td></td><td></td></tr>
<tr><td></td><td colspan="3">3. A single state agency must be established or designated to administer or designated to supervise the administration of the state plan.</td></tr>
<tr><td></td><td colspan="3">4. Methods of administration (other than those relating to select necessary for the efficient operation of the plan.
5. Reports must be submitted in such form and containing such required by the designated federal administrative agency.
6. Persons whose claims for assistance have been denied must be permitted an opportunity for a fair hearing before the state agency.</td></tr>
<tr><td></td><td colspan="2">7. State residence requirement may not exceed 5 years within last 9 years. One year of residence immediately preceding application may be required.
8. A state plan cannot impose any citizenship requirement which excludes any United States citizen.</td><td rowspan="2">7. State residence requirement must not disqualify a child who has resided in the state for a year immediately preceding application, or who was born in the state during the preceding year, if its mother has resided in the state for one year immediately preceding the birth.</td></tr>
<tr><td></td><td>9. After January 1, 1940, state plan must provide an age limit of not over 65 years, but until then a 70-year limit is permissible.
10. One-half of any recovery from estate of a recipient to be paid to the United States.</td><td>9. No aid to be given blind person while in receipt of old-age assistance under a federally approved plan.</td></tr>
</table>

APPENDIX

ACT RELATING TO FEDERAL GRANTS TO STATES

H.R. 7260]; Approved Aug. 14, 1935)

Maternal and child health (Secs. 501–505)	Crippled children (Secs. 511–515)	Child welfare (Sec. 521)	Public health (Secs. 601–603)
submitted by the state to the designated		The conditions are those involved in the purposes of the section: To enable the United States to cooperate with the states in establishing, extending, and strengthening, in predominantly rural areas, child-welfare services for the protection and care of homeless, dependent, and neglected children, and children in danger of becoming delinquent. The amounts shall be allotted on the basis of plans developed jointly by the Children's Bureau and state public-welfare agencies and be expended for payment of part of the cost of local services in areas predominantly rural, and for developing state services for the encouragement and assistance of adequate methods of community child-welfare organization in areas predominantly rural and other areas of special need.	The conditions are those involved in the purposes of the act, which are to assist states "in establishing and maintaining adequate public-health services, including the training of personnel for state and local health work." The moneys paid to any state must be used solely in carrying out these purposes and in accordance with plans presented by the state health authority to the Public Health Service.
plan (for each type of assistance, aid or			
minister the state plan or established or desig-			
For maternal and child-health services the state health agency must be used.			
tion, tenure, and compensation of personnel)			
Information as may be from time to time			
6. Provide for the extension and improvement of local maternal and child-health services administered by local child-health units.	6. Provide for carrying out the purposes specified in the appropriation.		
7. Provide for cooperation with medical, nursing, and welfare groups and organizations.	7. Provide cooperation with medical, health, nursing, and welfare organizations and with agencies charged with vocational rehabilitation of physically handicapped children.		
8. Provide for development of demonstration services in needy areas and among groups in special need.			

SUMMARY OF PROVISIONS OF THE SOCIAL SECURITY ACT

Provision	Old-age assistance (Secs. 1–6)	Aid to the blind (Secs. 1001–1006)	Aid to dependent children (Secs. 401–406)
Amount of federal grant to state.	One-half of state expenditures for assistance under each plan; but payments in excess of $30 a month to an individual are not matched by federal government. Five per cent of federal aid to state for administration and/or assistance under each plan.		One-third of state expenditures; but payments in excess of $18 per month for first child and $12 for each additional child are not matched by federal government.
Extent of state financial participation.	Amount equal to federal payment to state exclusive of federal 5 per cent.		Amount double federal payment to state.
Federal definition of aid.	Money payments to needy individual 65 years or older not an inmate of public institution.	Money payments to needy blind individual not an inmate of a public institution.	Money payments to needy dependent child or children under 16 years by reason of death, absence, or incapacity of a parent, living with an enumerated relative in a residence maintained as a home.
Method of making allotments.	Allotments made for each quarter on the basis of estimated state gations by the appropriate federal agency. Payments made to the state (at time or times fixed by the desig- sion) prior to audit or settlement by the General Accounting Office.		
Suspension of federal grant.	In the case of an approved plan which the Board finds after reasonable notice and opportunity for hearing has been changed to impose a prohibited requirement; or in the administration imposes a prohibited requirement with the knowledge of the state agency in a substantial number of cases, or fails to comply substantially with the provisions required in the plan, the Board shall notify the state agency that further payments will not be made.		
Federal agency	Social Security Board	Social Security Board	Social Security Board
Federal appropriation authorized—Fiscal year 1936.	$49,750,000	$3,000,000	$24,750,000

NOTE.—The Social Security Act also authorizes in Sec. 531 an appropriation of $841,- tation purposes, in addition to the appropriation available under the provisions of existing in the Department of the Interior. The Social Security Act also authorizes in Title III an states for the administration of their unemployment compensation laws.

APPENDIX

RELATING TO FEDERAL GRANTS TO STATES.—(*Continued*)

Maternal and child health (Secs. 501–505)	Crippled children (Secs. 511–515)	Child welfare (Sec. 521)	Public health (Secs. 601–603)
$20,000 to each state; and $1,800,000 distributed to the states in proportion to live births; and $980,000 distributed on basis of need, taking into consideration number of live births in state.	$20,000 allotted to each state and $1,830,000 distributed to the states on the basis of need taking into consideration the number of crippled children in need of such services and the cost thereof.	$10,000 alloted to each of the states and $990,000 distributed to the states not to exceed proportion of state to United States rural population.	$8,000,000 distributed to the states on the basis of (1) population, (2) special health problems, (3) financial needs.
Amount equal to federal payment to state exclusive of allotment on basis of need.	Amount equal to federal payment.	Not specifically provided in act.	Not specifically provided in act.
Services for promoting the health of mothers and children.	Services and facilities for crippled children or for children suffering from conditions which lead to crippling.	See above under "Conditions for approval of state plan."	See above under "Conditions for approval of state plan."
expenditures and appropriations, and investi-		Not specifically provided in act.	Allotments made for each quarter in accordance with regulations previously prescribed after conference with state health authorities.
nated federal agency) by the Secretary of the Treasury (through Disbursement Divi-			
In the case of an approved plan which the Secretary of Labor finds after reasonable notice and opportunity for hearing fails to comply substantially in the administration of the plan the Secretary shall notify the state agency that further payments will not be made.		Not specifically provided in act.	Not specifically provided in act.
Children's Bureau	Children's Bureau	Children's Bureau	Public Health Service
$3,800,000	$2,850,000	$1,500,000	$8,000,000

000 for the fiscal year 1936, to be distributed as grants to the states for vocational rehabili-
law; the Federal Vocational Rehabilitation Act is administered by the Office of Education
appropriation of $4,000,000 for the fiscal year 1936, to be distributed as grants to the

APPENDIX V

MAY 7, 1943 MEMORANDUM OF EVELINE M. BURNS LISTING HER SPEAKING ENGAGEMENTS FOR THAT MONTH

May 7, 1943

MEMORANDUM for Mr. George

Subject: Speaking engagements for May.

May

8 (Luncheon) Annual Meeting of League of Industrial Democracy, at 12:45 PM, Ball Room 24th Floor, Hotel McAlpin, New York City. Planning for Freedom from Want.

11 (Evening) Florida State Conference of Social Work, at 8:00PM. Address: Care of Miss Eileen Blackey, Chairman Program Committee, Angelbilt Hotel, Orlando, Fla. Planning for Freedom from Want.

13 (Afternoon) Address: Atlanta Field Office. Broadcast at 3:30 PM, Main Dining Room, Rich's Department Store. A Program on Social Security.

14 (Morning) Address: Atlanta Field Office. Will meet informally with group of student workers at Georgia School of Technology, teachers and students in social sciences from other educational institutions, professional social workers, Red Cross workers, etc. No formal speech.

14 (Luncheon) Address: Atlanta Field Office. Junior Chamber of Commerce. No formal speech.

17 (Evening) Pennsylvania School of Social Work, at 8:00 PM. Address: Care of Dr. Kenneth L. Pray, Director, 2410 Pine Street, Philadelphia, Pa. <u>The Security Report of the NRPB.</u>

19 (Evening) Annual Meeting of the Canadian Welfare Council, at 8:PM. Address: "Hold for" Dr. George F. Davidson, Executive Director, Royal York Hotel, Toronto, Canada. Title of address undecided.

21(Afternoon) United Neighborhood Houses of New York. Address: Mrs. V.G. Simkhovitch, University Settlement, 184 Elkridge Street, New York City. Title of speech undecided.

21 (Evening) New York School of Social Work, Alumni Association, 8:00 PM, at Town Hall. Address: Mr. Norman V. Lourie, Madison House, 226 Madison Street, New York City. <u>The American Security Report.</u>

28 (Morning) War Regional Meetings, of the National Conference of Social Work, at Cleveland, Ohio. Address: not quite clear - am writing today for details.

31 (Morning) Meredith College. Baccalaureate Address. Title still pending. Address: Mr. A.B. Cooper, Director of News Bureau, Meredith College, Raleigh, N.C.

Eveline M. Burns

cc: Miss Cain

BIBLIOGRAPHY

Books

Axinn, June, and Levin, Herman. Social Welfare: A History of the American Response to Need. 2nd ed. New York: Harper & Row, 1982.

Ball, Robert M. Social Security Today and Tomorrow. New York: Columbia University Press, 1978.

Burns, Eveline M. Toward Social Security: An Explanation of the Social Security Act and a Survey of the Larger Issues. New York: McGraw-Hill, 1936.

________. The American Social Security System. 2nd ed. Boston: Houghton Mifflin, The Riverside Press, 1951.

________. Social Security and Public Policy. New York: McGraw-Hill, 1956.

Cates, Jerry R. Insuring Inequality: Administrative Leadership in Social Security, 1935-54. Ann Arbor: University of Michigan Press, 1983.

Chambers, Clarke A. "An Historical Perspective on Political Action Vs. Individualized Treatment." In Perspectives on Social Welfare: An Introductory Anthology, pp. 89-106. Edited by Paul E. Weinberger. London: The Macmillan Company, Collier-Macmillan Limited, 1969.

Cohen, Wilbur J., and Friedman, Milton. Social Security: Universal or Selective? Washington, D.C.: American Enterprise Institute for Public Policy Research, 1972.

Dahl, Robert A. Who Governs? Democracy and Power in an American City. New Haven: Yale University Press, 1961.

Derthick, Martha. Policymaking for Social Security. Washington, D.C.: Brookings Institution, 1979.

Fisher, Jacob. The Response of Social Work to the Depression. Cambridge, Mass.: Schenkman Publishing Co., 1980.

Gil, David G. Unravelling Social Policy: Theory, Analysis and Political Action towards Social Equality. Cambridge, Mass.: Schenkman Publishing Co., 1973.

Gilbert, Neil, and Specht, Harry. Dimensions of Social Welfare Policy. Englewood Cliffs, N.J.: Prentice-Hall, Inc., 1974.

Heffernan, Joseph, and Turnan, Barbara. "Searching the Literature." In Social Work Research and Evaluation, pp. 46-56. Edited by Richard M. Grinnell, Jr. Itasca, Ill.: F. E. Peacock Publishers, Inc., 1981.

Heffner, Richard D. A Documentary History of the United States. Expanded ed. A Mentor Book. New York: New American Library, 1965.

Lindblom, Charles E. The Policy-Making Process. Foundations of Modern Political Science Series. Englewood Cliffs, N.J.: Prentice-Hall, Inc., 1968.

Myers, Robert. Social Security. 2nd ed. Bryn Mawr, Pa.: McCahan Foundation, 1981.

Patterson, James T. America's Struggle Against Poverty, 1900-1980. Cambridge, Mass.: Harvard University Press, 1981.

Perkins, Dexter. The New Age of Franklin Roosevelt, 1932-45. Chicago: University of Chicago Press, 1957.

Reisman, David A. Richard Titmuss: Welfare and Society. London: Heinemann, 1977.

Schlesinger, Arthur Meier. Political and Social Growth of the American People, 1865-1940. 3rd ed. New York: Macmillan, 1941.

Schlesinger, Arthur M., Jr. The Coming of the New Deal. Boston: Houghton Mifflin, 1959.

Shlakman, Vera. "Eveline M. Burns: Social Economist." In Social Security in International Perspective: Essays in Honor of Eveline M. Burns, pp. 3-25. Edited by Shirley Jenkins. New York: Columbia University Press, 1969.

Stein, Bruno. Social Security and Pensions in Transition. New York: Free Press, 1980.

Stuart, Paul. "Historical Research." in Social Work Research and Evaluation, pp. 316-332. Edited by Richard M. Grinnell, Jr. Itasca, Ill.: F. E. Peacock Publishers, Inc., 1981.

Witte, Edwin E. The Development of the Social Security Act. Madison: University of Wisconsin Press, 1962.

Reports, Papers, Articles

Advisory Council on Social Security. Social Security Financing and Benefits: Report of the 1979 Advisory Council. Washington, D.C.: Government Printing Office, 1979.

"The Aging of America." Congressional Quarterly Weekly Report 39 (28 November 1981): 2329-2346.

Brotman, Herman B. Every Ninth American. Prepared for the Special Committee on Aging, U.S. Senate. Washington, D.C.: Government Printing Office, 1980.

Burns, Eveline M. "Responsibility of Social Workers to Influence a Governmental Social Welfare Policy." Paper delivered at a workshop of the

1960 Alumni Conference of the Columbia University School of Social Work, 9 April 1960.

________. "Social Policy: The Stepchild of the Curriculum." In Proceedings of Ninth Annual Program Meeting, Council on Social Work Education, pp. 23-34. New York: Council on Social Work Education, 1961.

Clark, Lindley H., Jr. "Making Sense Out of Social Security: It's as Simple as A Plus B." Wall Street Journal, 24 July 1984.

Columbia University. Columbia Oral History Collection. 1948-

Consultants on Social Security. A Report to the Secretary of HEW on Extension of OASI to Additional Groups of Current Workers. Washington, D.C.: Government Printing Office, 1953.

Dunn, Loula. "Consultants' Report on Extension of OASI." Public Welfare 11 (October 1953): 115-118.

________. "Report to the Board of Directors for 1953." Public Welfare 12 (July 1954): 82-87.

________. "Report to the Board of Directors for 1954." Public Welfare 13 (July 1955): 87-94.

Gallup, George. "American Beveridge Plan Fails to Create Wide Public Stir in U.S." American Institute of Public Opinion press release, for release April 11 or 12, 1943. (Mimeographed.)

Herbers, John. "Rise of Elderly Population in 70's Portends Vast Changes in Nation." The New York Times, 24 May 1981.

Hoffman, David. "White House Rejects Foundation's Social Security Suggestions." Washington Post, 20 November 1984.

Humberger, Edward. "America's Elderly Poor." The Reporter 6 (May/June 1981): 39-47.

Kahn, Alfred J. "1978 Alumni Conference Address: Social Policy." Columbia University School of Social Work Alumni Newsletter (Winter 1978-1979): 5-7.

Levitt, Louis. "Social Work and Social Welfare: A Conceptual Matrix." Journal of Sociology and Social Welfare 7 (September 1980): 636-647.

Levy, Charles S. "The Social Worker as Agent of Policy Change." Social Casework 51 (February 1970): 102-108.

________. "(The Graduate) School (of Social Work) and Society." Journal of Education for Social Work 7 (Spring 1971): 25-30.

________. "Professional Ethics as Humanistic Ethics." Jewish Social Work Forum 9 (Spring 1972): 5-13.

________. "Putting the Social Work Back into Social Work." Journal of Jewish Communal Services 51 (Winter 1974): 171-178.

Lingg, Barbara A. Social Security Beneficiaries in Metropolitan Areas, 1979. Prepared for U.S. Department of Health and Human Services, Social Security Administration, Office of Research and Statistics. SSA Publication No. 13-11929. Washington, D.C.: Government Printing Office, 1981.

McNickle, Roma K. "Editorial Reaction to NRPB Security Report." (Mimeographed.)

National Association of Social Workers. The NASW Code of Ethics (as passed by the 1979 Delegate Assembly). Silver Spring, Md.: National Association of Social Workers, Inc.

National Commission on Social Security. Social Security in America's Future: Final Report of the National Commission on Social Security, March, 1981. Washington, D.C.: Government Printing Office, 1981.

Nelson, Gary. "Social Class and Public Policy for the Elderly." Social Service Review 56 (March 1982): 85-107.

Phillips, Norma Kolko. "Social Work, Government, and Social Welfare: The Social Security Act." D.S.W. dissertation, Wurzweiler School of Social Work, Yeshiva University, 1981.

President's Commission on Pension Policy. Coming of Age: Toward a National Retirement Income Policy. Washington, D.C.: Government Printing Office, 1981.

"Review & Outlook: The Untouchable." Wall Street Journal, 16 January 1985.

Rhine, Shirley H. America's Aging Population: Issues Facing Business and Society. A Research Report from The Conference Board. New York, 1980.

Schorr, Alvin L. ". . . Thy Father and Thy Mother . . .": A Second Look at Filial Responsibility and Family Policy. Prepared for U.S. Department of Health and Human Services, Social Security Administration, Office of Research and Statistics. SSA Publication No. 13-11953. Washington, D.C.: Government Printing Office, 1980.

Security, Work, and Relief Policies. Report of the Committee on Long-Range Work and Relief Policies to the National Resources Planning Board. Eveline M. Burns, Director of Research. Washington, D.C.: Government Printing Office, 1942.

Torrey, Barbara Boyle. Demographic Shifts and Projections: The Implications for Pension Systems. Working Paper prepared for the

President's Commission on Pension Policy [April 1979].

U.S. Congress. House. Select Committee on Aging. Aging in the World of Tomorrow (Part 1). Hearing before the Subcommittee on Federal, State and Community Services. Comm. Pub. No. 95-108. Washington, D.C.: Government Printing Office, 1977.

_________. _________. Omnibus Budget Reconciliation Act of 1981. Pub. L. 97-35, 97th Cong., 1st sess., 1981, H.R. 3982.

_________. _________. Social Security Amendments of 1983. Pub. L. 98-21, 98th Cong., 1st sess., 1983, H.R. 1900.

_________. _________. Select Committee on Aging. Tomorrow's Elderly. Report prepared by the Congressional Clearinghouse on the Future. Comm. Pub. No. 98-457. Washington, D.C.: Government Printing Office, 1984.

_________. Senate. Committee on Finance. The Social Security Act and Related Laws, November 1980 Edition (with December 1980 Revision Pages). Committee Print 97-2, 97th Cong., 1st sess., 1981.

U.S. Department of Health and Human Services. Office of Human Development Services. Administration on Aging. Facts about Older Americans 1979. Washington, D.C.: Government Printing Office, 1980.

_________. Health Care Financing Administration. Long Term Care: Background and Future Directions. Discussion paper. DHHS publication No. (HCFA) 81-20047. January 1981.

_________. Social Security Administration. Social Security Information Items, September 1981.

_________. _________. Social Security Bulletin, Annual Statistical Supplement, 1982.

Washington, D.C.: Government Printing Office, 1983.

U.S. Department of Health, Education, and Welfare. Social Security and the Changing Roles of Men and Women. Washington, D.C.: Government Printing Office, 1979.

________. Social Security Administration. Office of Research and Statistics. Income and Resources of the Aged. Washington, D.C.: Government Printing Office, 1980.

________. Report of the Universal Social Security Coverage Study Group. Washington, D.C.: Government Printing Office, 1980.

________. Social Security Administration. Social Security Handbook. Washington, D.C.: Government Printing Office, 1982.

U.S. Department of Labor. Bureau of Labor Statistics. Perspectives on Working Women: A Databook. Washington, D.C.: Government Printing Office, 1980.

Personal Communications

Interviews with Eveline M. Burns

12-13 June 1982; 7-8 August 1982; 18-19 June 1983; 15-16 January 1984; 26-27 May 1984.

Interviews, Correspondence, and Telephone Contacts with Social Work and Social Welfare Professionals Who Have Worked with Eveline M. Burns (Affiliation at Time of Contact)

Ball, Robert M. (Consultant on Social Security, Health, and Welfare Policy).

Bandler, Jean T. D. (New York University, School of Social Work, Faculty member).

Cohen, Wilbur (University of Texas at Austin, School of Social Work, Faculty member).

Katz, Arthur (Council on Social Work Education, Executive Director).

Merriam, Ida (Social Security Administration, Division of Research and Statistics, Retired).

Myers, Robert J. (Social Security Administration, former Chief Actuary, Retired).

Schorr, Alvin L. (Case Western Reserve University, School of Applied Social Sciences, Faculty member).

Shlakman, Vera (Columbia University, School of Social Work, Faculty member).

Weaver, Edward (American Public Welfare Association, Executive Director).

Wickenden, Elizabeth (Study Group on Social Security, Director).

INDEX